WORLD WAR II
IN MINUTES

R.G. GRANT

Quercus

Contents

Introduction

World War II was by far the largest-scale conflict in human history. Beginning at different times for different nations – 1937 for the Chinese, 1939 for Western Europeans, 1941 for the Russians and Americans – it ended in 1945 having caused the deaths of roughly one in thirty of the world's entire population.

Nothing about World War II was simple. It was not so much a single war as two separate conflicts that were only loosely connected. The first of those was a war between Britain, France, the United States and the Soviet Union on one side, and Nazi Germany and its European allies on the other, fought in Europe, North Africa and the Atlantic Ocean. The second was a conflict that pitted Japan against the United States, Britain and China, fought in the Pacific and Asia. These two wars were linked by the existence of a somewhat tenuous alliance between Germany and Japan, and by the involvement of America and Britain in both.

To give a clear, accessible account of a war of such complexity and gargantuan dimensions is no easy matter. This book follows a broadly chronological approach, from the causes of the war through to its consequences, but strict date order is necessarily disrupted by the need to follow the sequence of events in different parts of the world and give coherent accounts of major topics such as the strategic bombing of cities or Nazi genocide. Although the military campaigns that decided the outcome of the conflict necessarily receive most coverage, due attention is paid to social and political issues and to specific technological developments, from the first jet aircraft and ballistic missiles to chemical and nuclear weapons.

In one of his most famous speeches during World War II, British Prime Minister Winston Churchill suggested the outcome of the conflict would decide whether 'the life of the world may move forward into broad, sunlit uplands' or 'sink into the abyss of a new Dark Age'. If it is not possible now to present World War II as a straightforward contest between good and evil, it is still true that the hard-fought defeat of fascism and militarism has, to a large degree, determined the shape of the world in which we live today.

The war to end war

On 11th November 1918 an armistice ended the Great War, later renamed World War I. Fought between the major European powers, with a late intervention by the United States, the war exacted a shocking death toll – almost ten million military personnel killed – and ended with the defeat of Germany and its allies. It was British Prime Minister David Lloyd George who, attempting to justify this slaughter, called it 'the war to end war'. The conflict did indeed provoke a widespread longing for peace, but in practice its legacy was bitterness and instability. There was social and political upheaval in many countries, including a communist revolution in Russia and the overthrow of the monarchy in Germany. Some Germans refused to accept they had been militarily defeated, accusing German socialists and Jews of stabbing the army in the back. Among those who dreamed of reversing the verdict of the war was an ex-soldier, Adolf Hitler. As historian A J P Taylor wrote: 'The first war explains the second and, in fact, caused it, in so far as one event causes another.'

A scene from a front-line trench during World War I.

The Versailles Treaty

At the end of World War I the victorious powers held a peace conference in Paris. American President Woodrow Wilson envisaged a liberal settlement based on democracy and national self-determination. The French were more concerned to prevent any future German revenge attack. Britain and France had spent vast sums of money on the war and wanted to recoup the cost from the Germans. Under the terms of the Versailles Treaty, imposed without negotiation, Germany was largely disarmed and required to pay 'reparations'. It lost substantial territory, chiefly to Poland and France. A 'war guilt' clause declared Germany solely responsible for starting the war. The German government signed the treaty under duress, but almost all Germans were shocked by terms they saw as an unjust punishment. This view gained the support of opinion-formers in Britain and America so that, from an early stage among the victor powers, the will to uphold the treaty was weak. Other observers considered the terms too lenient. French general Ferdinand Foch said prophetically: 'This is not a peace. It is an armistice for twenty years.'

The Hall of Mirrors, Versailles, during the signing of the eponymous treaty.

The League of Nations

Established as part of the peace settlement at the end of World War I, the League of Nations embodied liberal aspirations to a peaceful future based on international cooperation. Members agreed to pursue disarmament and take collective action against any state guilty of aggression. Forty-two countries took part in the inaugural meeting in Geneva in 1920, but defeated Germany and revolutionary Russia were not among them. Nor was the United States. President Woodrow Wilson had promoted the League of Nations concept but US Congress refused to ratify the Versailles Treaty, worried that membership of the league might commit America to future foreign wars. Despite this evidence of American isolationism, progress with disarmament was made in the 1920s, especially in limitation of naval strengths. The admission of Germany to the league in 1926 marked a hopeful moment in the normalization of international relations. But when militarist powers rearmed and mounted acts of aggression in the 1930s, collective security would prove a delusion, the league capable only of futile gestures of disapproval.

THE GAP IN THE BRIDGE.

Published in the British satirical magazine, *Punch*, in 1919, this cartoon comments on the absence of the United States from the League of Nations.

Mussolini and the rise of Italian Fascism

Italy was among the victor powers in World War I, but emerged from the conflict in a state of political and social chaos. Almost 500,000 Italians had been killed with little gain to the country. Benito Mussolini was a former socialist journalist wounded in the war. The experience of warfare converted him to militarism and extreme nationalism. Arguing that only a dictatorship could save Italy from parliamentary corruption and left-wing revolution, Mussolini attracted a following of similarly discontented ex-soldiers whom he formed into a black-shirted militia called the Fasci di Combattimento. In summer 1922 Mussolini threatened to lead his blackshirts in a 'March on Rome' unless Italy's king Victor Emmanuel III appointed him head of government. The king caved in and made Mussolini prime minister. By 1926 Mussolini had established a single-party Fascist state that he ruled as 'Il Duce'. All opposition was crushed. Mussolini's example inspired militant nationalists in other countries hostile to liberal democracy. The term 'fascist' came to be applied in general to such movements, including the National Socialist Party in Germany.

Mussolini turns the March on Rome into a triumphant parade, having been made prime minister by the king.

The Weimar Republic

At the end of World War I a revolution created a democratic regime in Germany known as the Weimar Republic. The republic faced multiple problems from the outset, not least an economy that was in ruins. Both communists and right-wing militarists tried to overthrow the regime by force. Widely blamed for signing the hated Versailles Treaty, the Weimar government sought popular support through resisting payment of war reparations.

Events came to a head in 1923. When French and Belgian troops occupied the Ruhr industrial area to extract reparations, its workers went on strike as an act of resistance. The German government printed money to support them, but this led to hyperinflation. In 1924 an American-brokered deal rescheduled reparations payments. The German currency stabilized and American loans refloated the economy. With conservative war hero Paul von Hindenburg as president from 1925, Germany was readmitted to the international community. Unfortunately this normalization proved brief and illusory.

Hyperinflation reached phenomenal levels in the 1920s, with bank notes worth billions of marks in daily use.

Adolf Hitler

Austrian-born Adolf Hitler was a destitute failed artist when he joined the German Army as a volunteer at the start of World War I. He served in the trenches, rising to the modest rank of corporal. Like many soldiers he was shocked when Germany agreed an armistice in 1918. Bitter and resentful, he joined the National Socialist (Nazi) Party, one of several ultranationalist fringe groups in the Weimar Republic. An electrifying public speaker and a ruthless political operator, he turned the Nazis into a vehicle for his personal power.

In 1923 Hitler led a coup attempt in Munich, but the army remained loyal to the republic and he was arrested. In prison he wrote *Mein Kampf*, a personal life story expressing his political beliefs. It called for Germany to conquer *Lebensraum* ('room to live') in the Slav east and blamed the Jews for Germany's misfortunes. Released from prison in 1924, Hitler worked to achieve power through the ballot box. His long-term aim was to overthrow the Versailles Treaty and make Germany the dominant power in Europe.

Leading participants of the attempted coup in Munich in November 1923. Adolf Hitler stands fourth from the right.

The Great Depression

In October 1929 a sensational crash in share prices on the New York stock exchange triggered a global economic recession. In the years that followed, mass unemployment, collapsing banks and declining trade brought misery to millions. The Great Depression shook faith in liberal democracy and free trade. In many countries authoritarian government or dictatorship replaced parliamentary rule. In Germany, as unemployment rose to five million by 1931, voters turned to extremist parties – the Nazis on the right and the communists on the left. With the German parliament split into hostile blocs, a government appointed by President Hindenburg ruled by decree.

Countries raised trade barriers and devalued their currencies in an effort to save their own economies at the expense of those of others. Nationalists and militarists, notably in Japan and Germany, argued that the only path to economic security lay in direct control of territory and resources. Implying a division of the world into self-sufficient empires, this was a recipe for wars of conquest.

A poster from Germany's 1932 elections
declares Hitler to be 'Our Last Hope'.

Hitler comes to power

From 1928 Hitler campaigned tirelessly to make himself popular. His uniformed SA (*Sturmabteilung*) militia intimidated opposition on the streets, but otherwise he played by the democratic rules, arguing that the Versailles Treaty was the cause of the country's economic woes. The Nazis' vote share in Reichstag (government) elections peaked at 37 per cent in 1932, making them the largest group in a deadlocked parliament. In January 1933 President Hindenburg invited Hitler to head a government composed largely of traditional conservatives. Once in place as chancellor, Hitler exploited his powers. On the pretext of a fire that destroyed the Reichstag building in February, civil liberties were suspended. An Enabling Act was passed allowing Hitler to rule by decree. The Nazis were declared the sole political party, their opponents locked in concentration camps. In July 1934 Hitler won the support of the army through the bloody suppression of his unruly SA on the 'Night of the Long Knives'. After Hindenburg's death in August, a referendum confirmed Hitler's personal dictatorship as Führer (leader) of the Third Reich.

Deutsche, verteidigt Euch
gegen die jüdische
Greuelpropaganda,
kauft
nur bei Deutschen!

Germans defend
yourselves against jewish
atrocity propaganda
buy only at German shops!

A woman reads a boycott sign posted in the window of a Jewish-owned department store.

The Versailles Treaty overthrown

Germany had long sought to evade the terms of the Versailles Treaty, ducking reparations and conducting secret military training. Under Nazi rule covert development of the Luftwaffe (Germany's air force) was speeded up, but Hitler proceeded with caution. Although he withdrew from the League of Nations and from disarmament talks in 1933, it was not until March 1935 that he publicly announced rearmament, reintroducing conscription to expand the army to 600,000 men. Despite this blatant breach of the peace terms France failed to act, while the British even negotiated an agreement that legitimized German naval expansion.

By 1936 Hitler was ready for a serious gamble. The treaty banned Germany from stationing forces in the Rhineland, a part of Germany bordering on France. Sending troops into the area in March, Hitler knew any determined military response would force him to withdraw with fatal loss of face. But no resistance came. Britain and France had passively accepted the resurrection of Germany as a military power.

German troops enter the Rhineland to Nazi salutes from civilians.

Italy invades Ethiopia

Italian Fascist dictator Benito Mussolini nourished imperial ambitions. In October 1935 he launched an invasion of Ethiopia. Almost all of Africa was under European rule, so Mussolini saw no reason why his action should arouse objections. But Ethiopia was a member of the League of Nations and therefore theoretically protected by its principle of 'collective security'. Italian use of air power and mustard gas against the Ethiopians outraged public opinion. British and French diplomats, who were courting Mussolini as a potential ally against Germany, devised a peace deal favourable to Italy, but when this plan was leaked in December 1935, an outcry in the press forced it to be dropped. Instead Britain and France backed economic sanctions on Italy, imposed by the League of Nations. In May 1936 Ethiopian emperor Haile Selassie fled to exile in Britain. The League of Nations was discredited for having failed to prevent the victory of the Italian aggressors. Offended by the behaviour of the democracies, Mussolini signed a treaty with Hitler in October 1936, forming what the Italian dictator called 'the Rome-Berlin Axis'.

Fascist Party Secretary Lieutenant-General Achille Starace leads the occupation of the Lake Tana district of Ethiopia, April 1936.

The Spanish Civil War

In July 1936 nationalist army officers in Spain staged an uprising against the country's Republican government, a left-wing Popular Front coalition. Since the government kept control of key areas, including Madrid and Barcelona, a prolonged civil war ensued. The international impact of the conflict was immense. Fascist Italy and Nazi Germany sent air and ground forces to support the nationalists. The Soviet Union intervened militarily in support of the republic and volunteers from many countries fought in communist-organized international brigades. The British and French governments adopted a policy of non-intervention that, in practice, favoured the nationalists. Viewed internationally as a fight between fascism and its enemies, the conflict served as an ideological preparation for World War II. Whereas in the wake of World War I large sections of the left had embraced pacifism, the Spanish Civil War convinced most socialists of the need to arm to fight fascism. The eventual victory of General Francisco Franco in April 1939 condemned Spain to almost four decades of right-wing dictatorship.

A member of Spain's Unified Socialist Youth, Marina Ginestà was the longest-surviving French veteran of the Spanish Civil War, pictured here, in Barcelona at the start of the conflict.

Guernica

The most notorious single event of the Spanish Civil War was the bombing of the Republican-held Basque town of Guernica on 26th April 1937. The attack was carried out by aircraft of the German Condor Legion, the force sent by Nazi Germany to aid the Spanish nationalist rebels. Packed with people on market day, half of Guernica was reduced to ruins in three hours. The incident was widely publicized in the international press and memorialized by artist Pablo Picasso in a painting first exhibited at the World's Fair in Paris the following June. The bombing fed widely shared fears about the effect of German air power. It is now thought the death toll at Guernica was probably around 400, but initial estimates put the figure at almost 1,700. With other factors, this led the British authorities to calculate that, if war broke out with Germany, the Luftwaffe would inflict 150,000 civilian casualties on London in the first week of hostilities. Such exaggerated fears of destruction weighed heavily on British policymakers, undermining their will to stand up to Hitler.

The ruins at Guernica

China in turmoil

After World War I, China struggled to achieve coherent government. The nationalist Kuomintang movement, under Sun Yat-sen and his successor Chiang Kai-shek, battled against powerful regional warlords for control. A small but dedicated Chinese Communist Party, founded in 1921, initially allied itself with the Kuomintang. In areas of economic value, including Shanghai, foreign powers governed 'concessions'. Between 1926 and 1928, in a series of military campaigns known as the Northern Expedition, Chiang Kai-shek extended his rule over most of China. He also turned against the communists, massacring many of their activists. Survivors took refuge in remote rural areas. Escaping encirclement by Kuomintang forces in the Long March of 1934–35, the communists established themselves in Shaanxi province under the leadership of Mao Zedong.

Meanwhile, Japan, taking advantage of Chinese weakness, had begun a series of encroachments in the north. The Japanese occupied Manchuria in 1931 and pressed south towards Beijing.

Communists are rounded up in Shanghai
during a nationalist purge of April 1927.

The rise of Japanese militarism

When the young Emperor Hirohito ascended the throne in 1926, Japan was a parliamentary democracy and a member of the League of Nations. However, the military was not subject to the civilian government. When Prime Minister Hamaguchi Osachi tried to bring the military under civilian control in 1930, he was assassinated by a right-wing extremist. Radical nationalist ideas had taken root among junior officers, who aspired to making Japan a major imperialist power. In September 1931 army officers stationed in the South Manchuria Railway Zone, a Japanese concession in China, faked a Chinese attack on the railway at Mukden. This 'Mukden Incident' was used as a pretext for the Japanese army to occupy Manchuria, cheered on by a jingoistic press. Japan's civilian government was powerless to halt this military adventure. Condemned by the League of Nations, Japan quit the league in March 1933. Politicians remained at constant risk from right-wing terrorism, another prime minister assassinated by junior officers in 1932. With weak central leadership, Japan drifted towards a war for domination of China.

Victorious Japanese troops celebrate their invasion of Manchuria.

The Sino–Japanese War begins

China and Japan entered a confused state of semi-warfare. As Japan extended its hold over northern China there were outbreaks of severe fighting, notably around Shanghai in 1932, but Kuomintang leader Chiang Kai-shek was more concerned with defeating the Chinese communists. Anti-Japanese sentiment mounted in China, while Japan was increasingly tempted by the prospect of empire-building in Asia. In December 1936 Chiang Kai-shek was pressured into agreeing a loose alliance with the communists against the Japanese. Events came to a head in July 1937, when fighting broke out between Chinese and Japanese troops at the Marco Polo Bridge outside Beijing. This incident triggered an escalation to open warfare. From August to November a large-scale battle was fought at Shanghai. Casualties, both military and civilian, were heavy as fighting raged from street to street, with bombardment by Japanese aircraft and naval gunfire. Eventually the Japanese landed thousands of fresh troops, forcing the Chinese army to retreat. In retrospect, this could be seen as the first battle of World War II in Asia.

A terrified baby sits surrounded by destruction at Shanghai's South Station, bombed by the Japanese.

The Nanjing Massacre

After their victory at Shanghai, in December 1937 the Japanese occupied the Chinese Kuomintang capital Nanjing. What followed was one of the worst atrocities of the 20th century. Japanese troops engaged in a six-week orgy of rape and sadistic killing that left at least 50,000 Chinese civilians and military personnel dead. Instead of breaking the Chinese will to fight, the massacre inspired an enduring hatred of Japan. Regrouped around Wuhan, Chiang Kai-shek's forces fought in large battles through the summer of 1938. Chiang showed his ruthless determination by breaching the dykes of the Yellow River, flooding areas in the path of the Japanese advance at an uncounted cost in peasants' lives. Japanese forces succeeded in occupying all of eastern China, taking Wuhan and Canton in October, but the Kuomintang army continued resistance from a base at Chongqing, as did the Chinese communists further north around Yan'an. Japan set up puppet governments to rule areas of China under its control, but found itself committed to a protracted war that drained its limited financial and manpower resources.

Japanese occupation, 1938

- Japanese control
- Chinese communist control
- Chinese nationalist control

SOVIET UNION

MANCHUKUO

MONGOLIA

XINJIANG

Kaigan
Peking

Panyuan

Yan'an

QINGHAI

CHINA

Nanjing
Shanghai

JAPAN

TIBET

East
China
Sea

Kunming

TAIWAN

Canton

BURMA

South China Sea

FRENCH
INDOCHINA

HAINAN

PHILIPPINES

Anschluss and appeasement

German nationalists had long nurtured the desire to include Austria in a Greater Germany. On 12th March 1938 Hitler's troops crossed the Austrian border and occupied the country without a fight. In advance of the takeover Hitler had used the Austrian Nazi Party to undermine the country's government, but he had failed to extort an official invitation to send in troops. The Anschluss (annexation) was thus a clear act of aggression, as well as a breach of international treaties, yet Britain and France accepted it without protest. Since most Austrians were ethnically German, it was felt the principle of national self-determination justified Hitler's takeover. Neville Chamberlain, British prime minister from May 1937, was determined to avoid a war with Germany, both because of the catastrophic loss of life it would entail and because Britain was ill-equipped to fight. While pursuing rearmament, he decided to seek agreement with Hitler based on acceptance of Germany's 'legitimate demands' for a revision of its borders. This policy was dubbed 'appeasement'.

Hitler is greeted by cheering crowds in the Austrian capital Vienna following his occupation of the country.

The Munich crisis

C zechoslovakia, created by Czech nationalists in 1918, had a substantial ethnic German minority, chiefly in the Sudetenland border area. Encouraged by the Nazis, from spring 1938 the Sudeten Germans mounted a campaign for autonomy. This gave Hitler a pretext for a military attack on Czechoslovakia, planned to begin on 1st October. When British Prime Minister Chamberlain bullied the Czech government into making concessions, Hitler responded by increasing his demands. On 15th and 22nd September Chamberlain flew for meetings with Hitler in Germany but each time returned empty-handed. Britain and France reluctantly prepared for war. At the last moment, on 29th September, a four-power conference was arranged at Munich, Mussolini acting as intermediary. Hitler, Chamberlain, Mussolini and French premier Edouard Daladier agreed to impose a draconian solution on the Czechs, who were forced to hand the Sudetenland to Germany. Chamberlain returned to Britain declaring he had won 'peace in our time'. Privately Hitler was furious at being denied a war.

Chamberlain waves the Munich Agreement aloft in triumph.

Continued Nazi aggression

Chamberlain's appeasement policy was based on the assumption that Hitler was a rational politician with limited aims. But the irrational extremist nature of the Nazi regime was increasingly evident, and Hitler's goals did not change. He intended to achieve *Lebensraum* for the German people through the conquest of central and eastern Europe, win a war against the Western democracies, and impose a radical solution to the 'Jewish problem'. On 'Kristallnacht' (night of broken glass), 9th–10th November 1938, Nazi attacks on Jews across Germany and Austria destroyed synagogues, wrecked businesses and left 30,000 Jewish men in concentration camps. Then, in March 1939 Hitler's troops occupied the Czech capital, Prague. Czechoslovakia ceased to exist, divided into the pro-German state of Slovakia and the German-controlled Protectorate of Bohemia and Moravia. Finally convinced that only the threat of force would stop German expansion, the British government offered Poland a military guarantee against future German aggression. At the end of April Hitler told his generals to begin planning an invasion of Poland.

German troops march into the grounds of Hradcany Palace, Prague, after the occupation of Czechoslovakia in March 1939.

The Nazi–Soviet Pact

In 1919, to give newly independent Poland access to the sea, the Versailles peacemakers had allotted the Poles a strip of German territory, the Polish Corridor, and made the German port of Danzig (Gdansk) a Free City. In spring 1939 Hitler demanded the return of Danzig to Germany and a revision of the corridor. He correctly estimated that Poland's right-wing nationalist government would refuse, thus providing a pretext for an invasion. Desperate to avoid war, Britain and France continued to seek a compromise, while half-heartedly pursuing a rapprochement with Soviet dictator Joseph Stalin, whose military support would be essential if Poland was attacked. An Anglo-French military mission belatedly set off for Russia in August, but the Nazis acted faster. Foreign Minister Joachim von Ribbentrop flew to Moscow and hammered out a Non-Aggression Pact with the Soviets, signed on 23rd August. Its secret clauses allowed the Soviet Union a share in carving up Poland. This cynical alliance shocked the world, for Stalin and Hitler had been viewed as irreconcilable ideological enemies. It sealed Poland's fate.

German Foreign Minister Joachim von Ribbentrop (standing third from left) and Joseph Stalin (fourth) at the signing of the Nazi-Soviet Pact.

The war in Europe begins

In summer 1939 Hitler wanted a war with Poland, but not with Britain and France. The British and French governments also desperately wanted to avoid a war. A flurry of negotiations ensued in late August, while Hitler wavered about the timing of his long-planned invasion. Mussolini, who had signed a 'Pact of Steel' alliance with Germany the previous spring, contributed to Hitler's hesitation by telling him Italy was unprepared for war.

The British government was under pressure from public opinion to stand up to the Nazis. While urging the Poles to cede to Hitler's demands, Chamberlain confirmed Britain's commitment to Poland in the hope of deterring a German attack. Hitler decided to go ahead regardless. When German troops entered Poland on 1st September, the British and French governments still hesitated. Facing a mutiny in parliament, on 3rd September Chamberlain at last sent the Germans an ultimatum, France following suit. At 11.15 a.m. Chamberlain dolefully announced to the British people: 'This country is at war with Germany'.

German troops parade through Warsaw, Poland.

Evacuation

Expecting an outbreak of war to lead to immediate massively destructive air attacks on London and other cities, the British authorities had laid plans for the evacuation of schoolchildren. On 1st September 1939, two days before Britain's declaration of war on Germany, these plans were put into effect. Over three days some 1.5 million children and mothers with infants were evacuated to provincial towns and the countryside, where they were billeted upon householders deemed to have free space. The experience was eye-opening for all concerned. Some of the city children had never seen a cow; many of their hosts had never witnessed the effects of urban poverty. Around half the evacuees returned home within three months when the bombing failed to materialize.

In France, more than two million citizens were evacuated from border zones in early September. Emptied of its entire population, the city of Strasbourg became a ghost town. The arrival of a mass of evacuees from Alsace and Lorraine in rural southwest France was experienced as a serious culture clash.

Evacuees prepare to leave London for their countryside billets, 1939.

The defeat of Poland

On the night of 31st August 1939 the Nazis faked a Polish attack on a German radio station at Gleiwitz. Allegedly in response to this provocation, a full-scale German invasion of Poland was launched on 1st September. The Poles had a long indefensible border with Germany and were also attacked from Slovakia. Their air force was crippled by initial German air strikes, while German armies advanced from the north, west and south. By 13th September Warsaw, the Polish capital, was under siege. Polish forces regrouped in defensive positions behind the Vistula River, but on 17th September the Soviet Red Army invaded from the east. The Poles were incapable of fighting both the Nazis and the Soviets. Warsaw fell on 27th September and the last combat ended on 5th October. Nazi Germany and the Soviet Union divided Poland between them, instigating a reign of terror in their respective zones. Britain and France took no military action to aid the Poles. Although Hitler had denuded his western border of troops for the Polish operation, the French remained inertly on the defensive throughout.

The partition of Poland

The Phoney War

The six-month period after the defeat of Poland was dubbed the Phoney War for the lack of fighting. Britain and France refused to seek peace with Hitler but could not agree on offensive action. The French sat in their Maginot Line defences on their eastern border while a British Expeditionary Force (BEF) took up position in northern France. On the German side, Hitler horrified his generals by ordering an offensive against France to start in mid-November. The generals used the excuse of bad weather to have the operation repeatedly postponed. German air attacks on cities did not materialize. US President Franklin D Roosevelt had called on both sides to avoid bombing civilians, and no one wished to alienate America. British shipping suffered losses to magnetic mines and a German U-boat daringly sank the battleship *Royal Oak* in harbour at Scapa Flow. Otherwise most 'excess deaths' occurred through road accidents in cities 'blacked out' as an air-raid precaution – a problem soon much reduced by petrol rationing. As conscripts trained and arms production expanded, few doubted the real fighting would start soon enough.

A man stands guard in London to warn the city of air attacks.

The *Admiral Graf Spee*

The *Admiral Graf Spee* was a German cruiser with such powerful guns the British called it a 'pocket battleship'. Commanded by Captain Hans Langsdorff, in the opening months of the war the ship cruised the Indian Ocean and South Atlantic preying upon British merchant shipping. On 13th December 1939 a Royal Navy force consisting of the heavy cruiser *Exeter* and light cruisers *Ajax* and *Achilles* spotted the *Admiral Graf Spee* off the estuary of the Plate River, which separates Argentina and Uruguay. Despite being seriously outgunned, they unhesitatingly attacked. *Exeter* was crippled and forced to withdraw, but the *Admiral Graf Spee* also sustained damage, compelling Langsdorff to enter Montevideo harbour for repairs. Neutral Uruguay insisted the Germans leave port once repairs were completed or be interned for the duration. On 17th December, rejecting a showdown with British forces he wrongly believed to have arrived off Montevideo, Langsdorff scuttled his ship in the Plate River estuary. He shot himself two days later. This striking naval success boosted British morale in a depressing phase of the Phoney War.

The *Admiral Graf Spee*, scuttled off the coast of Montevideo.

The Winter War

Having absorbed eastern Poland in October 1939, Stalin turned his attention to the Baltic states and Finland. Estonia, Latvia and Lithuania agreed under duress to allow Soviet military bases on their territory, but the Finns refused. On 13th November the Red Army attacked Finland, starting what became known as the Winter War. Stalin intended to turn Finland into a communist puppet state but, under 72-year-old Commander-in-Chief Gustaf Mannerheim, the Finnish army fought with unexpected vigour. Poorly led and inadequately equipped, the Red Army failed to break through prepared defences. In a farcically irrelevant gesture, the Soviet Union was expelled from the League of Nations. British and French leaders drew up plans for an expeditionary force to aid the gallant Finns. This military adventure was forestalled by an improvement in the Red Army's performance under the fresh command of General Semyon Timoshenko. Their defences pierced, in March 1940 the Finns accepted a peace deal that left them independent but gave the Soviet Union the bases it had demanded.

A Finnish machine-gun nest 100 m (330 ft) from Soviet forces during the Winter War.

The battle for Norway

Although neutral, Norway and Sweden supplied vital iron ore to Germany via the Norwegian port of Narvik. To block this supply route the Allies planned to mine Norwegian coastal waters and possibly land troops at Narvik. Hitler was pursuing his own plans for the occupation of Norway, as a prelude to an offensive in France, and made his move just as the Allied mining began.

On 9th April German forces occupied Denmark without a fight and invaded Norway in an operation that included the first combat drop by paratroopers at Oslo. The Royal Navy was quickly on the scene and destroyed a significant percentage of the German surface fleet, notably in two battles at Narvik. However, British warships proved vulnerable to attack from land-based Luftwaffe aircraft. Belated landings of Allied troops around Trondheim in mid-April and at Narvik in early May were a chaotic failure. All surviving Allied troops had been evacuated by 8th June. The Germans took control of the country and a Royal Navy cruiser carried Norwegian King Haaken into exile in Britain.

Among the ships sent to defend Norway was the
aircraft carrier HMS *Ark Royal*, pictured here in 1940.

The German offensive in the West

On 10th May 1940 Hitler finally launched his Western offensive. Making decisive use of airborne forces, the Germans invaded the neutral Netherlands and forced the Dutch to surrender in four days after the devastating bombing of Rotterdam. A simultaneous invasion of neutral Belgium rapidly overcame border defences. Meanwhile, following a plan devised by General Erich von Manstein, the Germans pushed armoured columns into France through the poorly defended wooded hills in the Ardennes. Panzer tanks crossed the Meuse River at Dinant and Sedan on 13th May and drove towards the Channel, threatening to cut off Allied armies in northeastern France and Belgium. British and French forces launched counter-attacks but failed to stop the German advance, which had reached the Channel coast by 21st May. Three days later, on the advice of his cautious generals, Hitler ordered a pause in the armoured offensive, relying on the Luftwaffe to finish off the encircled Allied forces. The British began organizing an evacuation from the port of Dunkirk. The Belgians, isolated and completely outfought, surrendered unconditionally on 28th May.

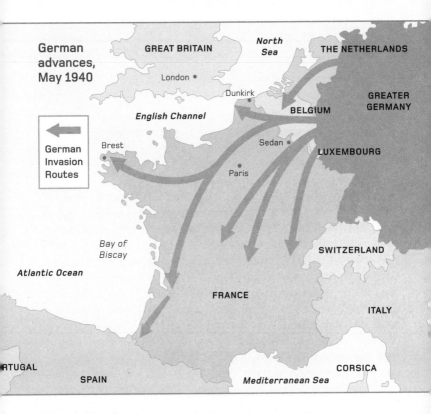

German advances, May 1940

GREAT BRITAIN

London

Dunkirk

English Channel

German Invasion Routes

Brest

North Sea

THE NETHERLANDS

GREATER GERMANY

BELGIUM

Sedan

LUXEMBOURG

Paris

Bay of Biscay

Atlantic Ocean

SWITZERLAND

FRANCE

ITALY

RTUGAL

SPAIN

CORSICA

Mediterranean Sea

The extent of the German advance into Western Europe, May 1940.

Blitzkrieg

The astonishing rapid victories of German forces in spring 1940 were not achieved through superior numbers or quality of equipment. Even the best German tanks, Panzer IIIs and Panzer IVs, were in some ways inferior to Allied equivalents. The Junkers Ju-87 Stuka dive-bomber, the key German ground-attack aircraft, was slow and vulnerable to enemy fighters. The root of German success lay not in technology but in tactics. The essential features of *Blitzkrieg* (lightning war) were shock and momentum. A powerful punch delivered by columns of tanks and motorized infantry at a weak point in the enemy's defences created a breakthrough that was exploited at speed. The mobile columns penetrated in depth, supported by Stukas acting as a substitute for artillery. The action of combined arms was coordinated by radio, while airborne forces served to seize key strongpoints or enemy airfields. *Blitzkrieg* tactics were always risky because the breakthrough columns could be cut off or outrun their supplies, but they succeeded against soldiers with shaky morale fighting under mediocre commanders incapable of reacting with speed.

Columns of Panzer III tanks and motorized
infantry advance at speed in southern Russia.

Churchill becomes British prime minister

After the outbreak of war Chamberlain remained British prime minister but there was mounting discontent at his failure to pursue the war with sufficient energy. Brought into the government as First Lord of the Admiralty, Winston Churchill enhanced his reputation through the relatively active role of the navy during the Phoney War. He was known as a consistent opponent of Hitler, whereas Chamberlain was compromised by appeasement. The failings of the Norway campaign brought discontent to the boil. After a Conservative backbench revolt in the House of Commons on 8th May 1940, Chamberlain's position became untenable. King George VI would have liked foreign secretary Lord Halifax as prime minister, but it was evident only Churchill could command sufficient support. On 10th May, the same day the German Western offensive began, Churchill was sworn in as prime minister, forming a coalition government with Labour leader Clement Attlee as his deputy. 'I felt as if I were walking with destiny,' Churchill later wrote, 'and that all my past life had been but a preparation for this hour and for this trial.'

Churchill's coalition government, with Churchill seated
fourth from the right and Clement Attlee to his right.

Winston Churchill

The new British prime minister was a maverick politician with a chequered record. Churchill was disliked by socialists for allegedly using troops against striking workers when home secretary in 1910. In World War I he had been responsible for the disastrous Gallipoli expedition. In the 1930s he had made himself unpopular by opposing Indian self-rule and supporting Edward VIII in the abdication crisis. Yet his advocacy of rearmament and resistance to Hitler, often dismissed as warmongering at the time, came to seem prescient in retrospect. Facing the House of Commons on 13th May 1940, the new premier offered only 'blood, toil, tears and sweat' in pursuit of 'victory at all costs'. It was this single-minded sense of purpose, expressed in thrilling rhetoric, that was to carry Britain through the darkest days of the war. As head of the War Cabinet and Minister of Defence, Churchill exercised a preponderant control over military decision-making. Many of his decisions would turn out to be wrong. But he inspired the war effort with an energy and willpower no one else could have matched.

The evacuation at Dunkirk

On 26th May 1940 the British launched Operation Dynamo, an attempt to evacuate encircled Allied soldiers through the French port of Dunkirk. As the German army resumed its offensive after the pause ordered in May, a defensive perimeter around the town was held in fierce fighting, while troops boarded warships for transport across the English Channel. The Luftwaffe launched repeated air attacks that fighter aircraft of the British Royal Air Force (RAF) vainly strove to hold off. A flotilla of small civilian boats was mobilized to aid in the evacuation, ferrying men from the beaches around Dunkirk to larger vessels offshore. By 3rd June, when German troops captured the port, some 200,000 British and 140,000 French soldiers had been brought to England. This miraculous escape could not disguise the scale of the military disaster. The British Expeditionary Force had left behind all its tanks and guns. The Allied navies had lost nine destroyers, mostly sunk by bombing, and the RAF also suffered heavily. Although British propagandists lauded the courage and heroism of the operation, Churchill commented succinctly: 'Wars are not won by evacuations'.

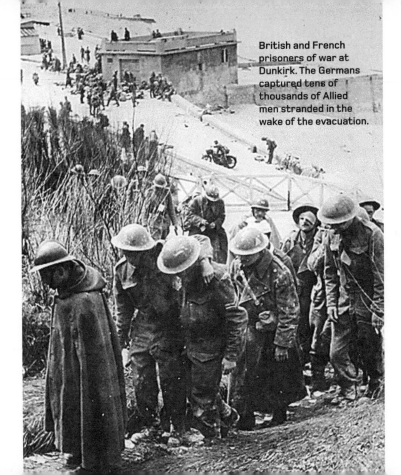

British and French prisoners of war at Dunkirk. The Germans captured tens of thousands of Allied men stranded in the wake of the evacuation.

The defeat of France

After the Dunkirk evacuation the battle for France continued. On 5th June 1940 the Germans launched a new offensive on the Somme and the Aisne. There were still British troops in France and more were sent. French soldiers continued fighting valiantly against increasingly adverse odds, but French Commander-in-Chief General Maxime Weygand, a man of right-wing sympathies, was infected with defeatism. While Prime Minister Paul Reynaud, who had replaced Daladier in March, remained resolutely in favour of continued resistance, Weygand demanded an armistice. As German forces advanced on Paris, the French government retreated, first to Tours, and then Bordeaux. Most of the city's population also fled. German troops occupied Paris on 14th June. Two days later Churchill proposed a Franco-British Union to continue the war. Reynaud would have accepted and carried on fighting from French North Africa, but he was opposed by his cabinet and resigned. With German armies advancing almost unchecked across France, the new prime minister, Marshal Philippe Pétain, requested an armistice.

A Frenchman weeps as German soldiers march into Paris, on 14th June 1940.

The French surrender

On 22nd June France signed a humiliating armistice agreement with Germany. The ceremony was staged in the same railway carriage where the defeated Germans had signed an armistice in 1918. The surrender terms divided France into Occupied and Unoccupied zones. The Germans took direct control of the north and west, leaving the French government to run the southeast.

Establishing themselves in the spa town of Vichy, Pétain and his supporters, including the skilled politician Pierre Laval, exploited the opportunity offered by defeat to pursue a long-nourished right-wing agenda. The democratic Third Republic was abolished as Pétain became both head of state and government in a conservative Catholic authoritarian regime, employing the slogan: 'Work, Family and Fatherland'. The Vichy government hoped to become accepted as a loyal colleague of Nazi Germany. Meanwhile Charles de Gaulle, a little-known officer who had escaped to exile in London, broadcast an appeal to the French people calling for continued resistance. In the hour of defeat, few listened.

Hitler in Paris. In spectacular fashion, Hitler had achieved his goal of reversing the verdict of World War I.

Britain attacks the French fleet

Vichy France remained in control of the French colonial empire and of the powerful French fleet, mostly stationed in the Mediterranean. Britain sought to prevent the French warships ending up in German hands, which would have fundamentally altered the naval balance of power. French naval chief Admiral François Darlan promised his ships would never be handed to the Germans, but Churchill believed the matter too important to be trusted to a promise. In early July the British moved to take over all French warships they could reach. A Royal Navy fleet was sent from Gibraltar to the major naval base of Mers el-Kébir in French Algeria. The French naval commander Admiral Gensoul refused to bow to British demands, so the British attacked the French fleet in harbour. Naval gunfire and strikes by carrier aircraft sank the battleship *Bretagne* and severely damaged five other warships. Almost 1,300 French sailors were killed. France retaliated with ineffectual air raids on Gibraltar, but the Vichy regime stopped short of declaring war on Britain. Nonetheless, anti-British feeling ran high among the French people.

British attacks on the French fleet at Mers el–Kébir, 3rd July 1940.

The Battle of Britain

On 16th July 1940 Hitler ordered preparations for an invasion of Britain. Both sides saw command of the air as crucial. The conquest of France and Belgium had given the Luftwaffe bases within easy reach of southern England. The German pilots and aircraft were capable of outfighting the RAF, but Hitler's aviation chief Hermann Goering lacked a coherent strategy. Led by Air Chief Marshal Hugh Dowding, RAF Fighter Command consistently sought to conserve its strength while denying the Luftwaffe control of the air. At first, aerial combat took place over the English Channel and Britain's southern ports; the Luftwaffe began a major assault on RAF airbases, aircraft factories and radar stations on 13th August. Using fleets of bombers with fighter escorts, this campaign seemed close to crippling British air defences when, on 7th September, the Germans switched to mass daylight bombing raids on London. Heavy losses inflicted on German bombers on 15th September were hailed by the British as the climax of what became known as the Battle of Britain. In October the Luftwaffe gave up daylight raids, admitting failure to establish command of the air.

German Heinkel He-111 aircraft fly over the English Channel.

British air defences

The first battle fought exclusively in the air, the Battle of Britain was a stiff test of the air-defence system developed by the British in time for World War II. This depended on radar, a technology developed in the 1930s. Radar stations on the coast provided warning of incoming aircraft that was conveyed to control rooms, where women of the Auxiliary Air Force represented aerial movement by pushing blocks around a map. Air controllers ordered fighter squadrons to 'scramble' and directed them on to their targets. The RAF had two excellent fighter aircraft, the Supermarine Spitfire and the Hawker Hurricane, but a severe shortage of experienced pilots, making it dependent on fliers from the Commonwealth and Occupied Europe, such as Czechs and Poles. The Luftwaffe's fleets of bombers were escorted by Messerschmitt Bf 109 fighters flying at high altitude. The RAF pilots' job was to attack the bombers without getting 'bounced' by the diving Bf 109s. Although figures are disputed, the three-month battle was roughly even, with around 1,700 RAF aircraft destroyed to 2,000 of the Luftwaffe.

As many as 370 Supermarine Spitfires (pictured) and 700 Hawker Hurricanes faced the Luftwaffe during the Battle of Britain.

The invasion that never was

Although former appeasers in the British government favoured negotiations with Hitler after the fall of France, Churchill was determined to fight on and won general support for his stance. Hitler hinted at a possible peace deal but prepared an invasion of Britain, Operation Sea Lion, scheduled for mid-September 1940. The Churchill government took measures to meet the emergency. Enemy aliens – civilians from hostile countries – were rounded up and sent to internment camps. Over a million volunteers were enrolled in the Home Guard, a poorly armed auxiliary force. Road signs were removed and ringing of church bells was banned – to be rung only to signal the invasion. Plans were made to use poison gas against the invaders on the beaches. Meanwhile the Germans converted thousands of river barges into improvised landing craft. Assembled at Channel ports, they were to land troops at coastal sites across southern England. There were also to be airborne landings by paratroopers. But the invasion never happened. Lacking command of either the air or the sea, Hitler postponed the operation on 17th September and it was quietly abandoned.

Members of the House of Lords and the House of Commons, many of them experienced soldiers and veterans of the last war, train as members of the local defence volunteers, in London, England.

Chemical warfare

Combatant countries manufactured varieties of poison gas on a large scale during World War II, yet these chemical arsenals remained mostly unused. Britain intended to deploy mustard gas and phosgene to repel a German invasion in 1940, but the invasion never came. Churchill on occasion urged the use of gas against German cities but was resisted by his military chiefs. When American military leaders wanted to use gas against the Japanese in the Pacific, Roosevelt refused permission. Both Britain and America fully intended to resort to chemical warfare if their enemies did.

The Germans possessed not only poison gas but also newly developed nerve agents – tabun, sarin and soman. Yet for reasons that are unclear, Hitler, who gassed millions in death camps, never deployed these deadly agents on the battlefield. The sole significant loss of life to chemical weapons in Europe occurred at Bari, Italy, in December 1943 when an American ship carrying mustard gas was hit in a German air raid.

Only the Japanese made extensive military use of poison gas during World War II, against the Chinese. Here, Japanese troops wear gas masks as they prepare for an advance in Shanghai, China, 1937.

The Blitz

From September 1940 to May 1941 British cities were subjected to sustained aerial bombing that killed around 40,000 civilians. Although dwarfed by the scale of Allied strategic bombing later in the war, it was at the time the most extreme use of airpower ever seen. From October 1940, when the Luftwaffe switched from day to night attacks, Britain had no defence. Anti-aircraft guns and night fighter aircraft were largely ineffectual. Fortunately for the British, Germany had failed to develop a four-engine heavy bomber. The campaign was conducted by Junkers Ju-88s, Heinkel He-111s and Dornier Do-17s, aircraft carrying relatively modest bombloads. Nonetheless, a mix of high-explosive and incendiary devices caused massive damage to London and other cities, including Hull, Liverpool, Belfast, Plymouth, Coventry and Glasgow. Germany's objective was never clear. The bombers attacked industrial and economic targets, yet Nazi Air Chief Goering sometimes spoke as if the bombing would terrorize the British into surrender. The Blitz ended in spring 1941 when Hitler transferred his aircraft eastward to prepare for an invasion of the Soviet Union.

London's St Paul's Cathedral rises above the smoke and flames on one of the worst nights of bombing experienced in Britain, 29th December 1940.

The destruction of Coventry

The devastating Luftwaffe attack on the industrial town of Coventry on the night of 14th–15th November 1940 exemplified the effectiveness of German night-bombing. To locate targets in blacked-out Britain, the Luftwaffe used radio navigation techniques developed for civilian flights before the war. The bombers, consisting of a pathfinder group of a dozen Heinkel He-111s, followed the line of a directional radio beam sent from a transmitter in Brittany. As they approached the target they picked up 'crossbeams' sent from other radio transmitters, which told them exactly when to release their incendiary bombs. A fleet of several hundred bomber aircraft following behind were guided to their target by the fires lit by the pathfinders. The British made efforts to block the German radio transmissions, but in this case without success. Much of Coventry was destroyed, with the loss of some 500 lives. The effectiveness of the Luftwaffe contrasted with the clumsy efforts of RAF Bomber Command, whose attempts at night-bombing of Germany in 1940–41 failed because, flying blindly in the darkness, they rarely found their targets.

The ruined nave and chancel of Coventry Cathedral, England, seen from the west tower.

Surviving the bombing

During the Blitz, London was bombed for a total of 57 nights, with severe destruction to the City and the poor districts of the East End. The government had distributed Anderson shelters, flimsy structures that could be erected in back gardens, and provided some communal shelters. Sirens warned of the approach of the bombers, while air-raid wardens policed the blackout – a collective minimizing of visible light at nighttime. Volunteer fire watchers were stationed on the roofs of buildings to respond to incendiary attacks. Fire and ambulance services were at times stretched to breaking point and beyond.

Yet far fewer people moved out of London than in the original evacuation at the start of the war. There was looting of the ruined buildings but also comradeship in shared suffering, and overall the bombing increased the resolve to fight. It was indicative of the popular mood that Churchill or members of the royal family were warmly greeted when they walked through bombed-out streets after raids.

One in seven Londoners slept in the city's Underground stations during the Blitz.

U–boat warfare in the Atlantic Ocean

Britain was dependent on imports of food, fuel and war material by sea. After the fall of France the German U-boat (submarine) fleet, commanded by Admiral Karl Dönitz, was shifted from Germany to bases in Brittany, from which it could prey upon Atlantic convoys. The Royal Navy had too few ships suitable to escort merchant convoys and placed too much faith in Asdic, a device that detected submarines under water. Dönitz ordered the U-boats to evade Asdic by attacking on the surface at night. Gathering to form 'wolf packs', the U-boats penetrated the escort screen and wrought havoc upon slow-moving merchant ships with their torpedoes. In October 1940, 32 merchant ships were sunk in one five-day period. U-boat commanders such as Otto Kretschmer, Günther Prien and Joachim Schepke were celebrated by Nazi propagandists as 'aces', their 'scores' publicized. By spring 1941, however, Britain was mounting a fight back, with more escort vessels and the effective use of patrol aircraft. Kretschmer, Prien and Schepke were all killed. The U-boat menace remained, but for U-boat crews the 'Happy Time' was over.

A German U-boat rides the waves, painted by Augusto Ferrer-Dalmau

The sinking of the
Bismarck

In May 1941 the newly built German battleship *Bismarck*, accompanied by the cruiser *Prinz Eugen*, sailed from the North Sea into the Atlantic to raid British merchant convoys. Encountering the Royal Navy battleship *Prince of Wales* and the cruiser *Hood* in the Denmark Strait, east of Greenland, *Bismarck* sank the *Hood* with the loss of all but three crew. As the German battleship's fuel tanks had been damaged in the exchange of fire, she headed for safety in Brittany while the *Prinz Eugen* continued with commerce-raiding. The Royal Navy assembled all available resources to hunt for the *Bismarck*. Spotted near France in the North Atlantic by a patrolling flying boat on 26th May, the German battleship was intercepted by a force that included the carrier *Ark Royal*. Attacked by carrier aircraft – Fairey Swordfish biplanes known affectionately as 'Stringbags' – the *Bismarck* was hit by two torpedoes. Out of control, it was battered by the guns of two Royal Navy battleships, *King George V* and *Rodney*, and finally sunk by torpedoes from the cruiser *Dorsetshire*.

Survivors from the *Bismarck* are pulled aboard HMS *Dorsetshire*, 27th May 1941. Only 110 of a crew of more than 2,000 survived.

Enigma and Bletchley Park

All combatants in World War II used radio for communication. Since anyone could pick up messages, it became vital to defend secrecy through the use of codes. The Enigma machine, developed in the 1920s, was an electro-mechanical means of enciphering and deciphering messages. Variants of the machine were adopted by all the German armed services, who believed Enigma codes could not be cracked. However, Polish intelligence services had made considerable progress with deciphering Enigma messages in the 1930s and shared their information with Britain and France at the start of World War II. The British established a code-breaking centre at Bletchley Park in Buckinghamshire, which provided a stream of valuable intelligence known as Ultra. Decoding was never straightforward, as the settings for the Enigma machines were changed every day. Success depended on failings in German security procedures, such as the repetition of standard elements in messages. To avoid alerting the Germans to the breach of their codes, the circulation of Ultra intelligence was severely restricted, which to a degree limited its usefulness.

An Enigma cipher machine on display inside the
Museum of the Second World War, Gdansk, Poland.

Britain's 'war socialism'

To face the wartime emergency, the British government assumed unprecedented powers. The allocation of labour and the production, consumption and distribution of goods were all controlled. Petrol was severely rationed, as were scarce foodstuffs. 'Utility' rules were imposed on the manufacture of clothing and furniture to cut use of raw materials. The Ministry of Labour could direct 'any person to perform any service required in any place', for instance drafting young men to work in coal mines. From 1941 unmarried women under the age of thirty were conscripted into the armed forces or to war work – a measure later extended to women up to fifty. Equality of sacrifice was seen as vital for social cohesion and luxury spending was discouraged – as when a limit was set on how much could be spent on a restaurant meal. Issued in 1942, the Beveridge Report, prefiguring the postwar welfare state, was welcomed with enthusiasm. Increased taxation to finance the war and rising industrial wages sharply reduced the income gap between the middle and working classes. This 'war socialism' was to have a profound effect on Britain's future.

Eleanor Roosevelt talks to a woman machinist during her goodwill tour of Great Britain, November 1942.

Italy enters the war

Despite its Pact of Steel alliance with Nazi Germany, at the outbreak of World War II Italy remained neutral. Mussolini was too aware of the weakness of his country's economy and the backwardness of its armed forces to attempt a war against Britain and France. Hitler's lightning victories in spring 1940 changed everything. With the French on the brink of defeat, on 10th June Mussolini declared war on the Allies, launching an opportunist attack on southeast France. The fighting soon ended, leaving Italy in occupation of a French border zone. Mussolini embarked upon the grandiose project of making Italy the dominant power in the Mediterranean. In July his forces in Libya, an Italian colony, invaded Egypt. The Italians vastly outnumbered the British forces protecting the naval base at Alexandria and the Suez Canal, but their advance was indecisive. Despite Britain's dire military plight, Churchill sent 150 tanks to defend Egypt. In late October Mussolini opened war on another front, invading Greece from Albania. It would prove too much for poorly equipped, badly led Italian armies.

An Italian L3–35 tankette. The small, light tanks proved inadequate for modern warfare, having too thin armour and weak armament of only machine guns.

British victories over Italy

On 9th December 1940 General Sir Archibald Wavell, the British commander in the Middle East, launched an attack on Italian forces in Egypt. His desert army consisted of the British 7th Armoured Division, later dubbed the 'Desert Rats', and chiefly Indian and Australian infantry. Taken by surprise, the Italians were soon in headlong retreat. The Australian troops took the Libyan port of Tobruk on 22nd January 1941. In early February the British advanced on Benghazi, where a bold manoeuvre by 7th Armoured Division trapped the retreating Italians at the battle of Beda Fomm.

Meanwhile another Italian disaster was taking place in East Africa, where both Britain and Italy had colonial territories. During 1940 the Italians launched ineffectual incursions into British Somaliland and Sudan. Taking the offensive in January 1941, the British rapidly occupied Eritrea, Italian Somaliland and Ethiopia. Ethiopian Emperor Haile Selassie, driven into exile by Mussolini's forces in 1936, triumphantly re-entered his capital Addis Ababa on 5th May.

Italian prisoners of war. The British captured more than 100,000 Italians during their 1940–41 campaign in Africa.

Naval war in the Mediterranean

Italy's navy, the Regia Marina, was in better fighting shape than its army, but it lacked modern equipment, including radar. Supported by land-based aircraft, Italian warships threatened the sea route between Britain's bases at Gibraltar and Alexandria. The Royal Navy chose to attack. On the night of 11th–12th November 1940, Swordfish biplanes from the carrier *Illustrious*, armed with bombs and torpedoes, struck the Italian fleet in harbour at Taranto, crippling three battleships. The raid was a striking demonstration of the effectiveness of naval aviation and partly inspired Japan's 1941 attack on Pearl Harbor. Any possibility the Italian surface fleet might dominate the Mediterranean ended the following spring. On the night of 28th–29th March 1941 a British force, including three battleships and a carrier, commanded by Admiral Sir Andrew Cunningham, intercepted an Italian fleet off Cape Matapan, Greece. The Italians were neither equipped nor trained for night fighting. In pitch darkness five Italian ships were sunk and the battleship *Vittorio Veneto* was damaged. The Italian navy never sortied again in fleet strength.

Swordfish biplane

Rommel leads the Afrika Korps

Needing to rescue his Italian allies from defeat in the Desert War (the campaign in North Africa), in February 1941 Hitler sent General Erwin Rommel to Libya at the head of an armoured expeditionary force, the Afrika Korps. Originally an infantry officer, Rommel had demonstrated his flair for aggressive tank warfare in the battle for France. Arriving in North Africa, he had the good fortune to face British forces weakened by the diversion of troops to Greece. The Afrika Korps' tanks easily outfought those of their opponents. A probing attack launched in March developed into a full-scale offensive that drove the British back into Egypt in disarray. The 9th Australian Division was left surrounded at the port of Tobruk, far behind the new Axis frontline. Resupplied by sea, the Australians held a defensive perimeter through six gruelling months. British counter-attacks in May (Operation Brevity) and June (Operation Battleaxe) failed to break through. In October the exhausted Australians were replaced by British troops who held the port until the siege was finally lifted in early December.

General Erwin Rommel with the 15th Panzer Division between Tobruk and Sidi Omar.

Germany overruns the Balkans and Greece

Mussolini's decision to invade Greece in October 1940 led as swiftly to disaster as his operations in North Africa. Through the following winter the Italians suffered humiliating setbacks against an enemy they had expected to overcome with ease. With the fighting stalemated, Greece appealed for support from Britain while Mussolini appealed to Hitler.

In March Britain began moving an expeditionary force into Greece, while Germany pressured Bulgaria and Yugoslavia into joining the Axis alliance. The signing of the alliance provoked a coup in Yugoslavia, however, a new government reversing the decision to join the Axis. Hitler responded by launching a devastating offensive against both Yugoslavia and Greece on 6th April. Italian and Hungarian forces joined in the German attack on Yugoslavia, which brought the Yugoslav army to unconditional surrender in ten days. The subjugation of Greece took three weeks. The survivors of the defeated British expeditionary force were evacuated from the Greek mainland to the island of Crete.

German soldiers hoist the Swastika at the Parthenon in Athens, Greece, 14th May 1941.

The airborne invasion of Crete

After Axis forces occupied Greece in April 1941, General Karl Student, the commander of German airborne forces, won Hitler's backing for an assault on Crete by parachute troops. The airborne attack was to be supported by seaborne landings. The British were forewarned of this operation by Ultra intelligence, but the Allied commander on the island, New Zealand General Bernard Freyberg, underrated the airborne element, convinced the main attack would come by sea.

The airborne assault was launched on 20th May. By the day's end, despite heavy losses on arrival, the Germans had control of Maleme airfield and were able to fly in reinforcements. The Royal Navy prevented German troops arriving by sea, but those delivered by air sufficed to defeat demoralized Allied soldiers fighting without air cover. An evacuation mounted under constant air attack rescued 16,000 men by the time the island fell on 1st June. The battle for Crete cost the Royal Navy three cruisers and six destroyers sunk by the Luftwaffe.

German aeroplanes land troops on Crete, 1941. Landing by parachute or glider within sight of Allied troops, the Germans were easy targets.

The siege of Malta

The British naval base on Malta threatened Axis supply routes to North Africa, but although the island was only 100 km (60 miles) from Sicily, neither the Italians nor the Germans were prepared to attempt an invasion, daunted by the heavy losses such an operation would entail. Instead they resorted to air attack and naval blockade in an effort to force Malta to surrender.

The Italians had been bombing Malta since entering the war, but air attacks began in earnest when the Luftwaffe sent units to Sicily in January 1941. The RAF stationed substantial numbers of fighters on Malta. Although they could not prevent the bombing, they forced the Axis to turn to night attacks. Merchant convoys carrying supplies to the island suffered heavy losses to air attack and, in 1942, the surrounding waters were mined, almost blocking access. Food supplies ran perilously low. Relief only came from November 1942, when Allied victories in North Africa changed Axis military priorities and took the pressure off Malta. The entire island was awarded the George Cross for bravery.

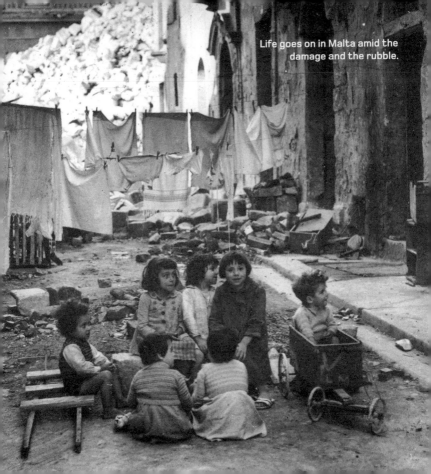
Life goes on in Malta amid the damage and the rubble.

The Desert War: from Crusader to Alam Halfa

The Desert War was fought between the British Eighth Army, a multinational force including Commonwealth, Free French and Polish troops, and Rommel's German and Italian Panzerarmee Afrika. In November–December 1941 the British Operation Crusader forced Rommel to withdraw deep into Libya. But the following spring he returned to the offensive, attacking the Eighth Army defensive line at Gazala. Beginning on 26th May, Italian infantry made a frontal assault on the defences while German tanks carried out an encircling move to the south. Despite heroic resistance by the Free French at Bir Hakeim, the panzers broke through. British armour attempting a counter-attack were savaged by German 88mm guns, the war's most effective anti-tank artillery. Driven back in disarray, the British reformed at El Alamein in Egypt. Rommel's path seemed open to the Suez Canal, but his forces ran short of fuel and munitions. He failed to break through British defences at the First Battle of Alamein in July and again at the Battle of Alam Halfa in August–September. That proved the last Axis offensive of the Desert War.

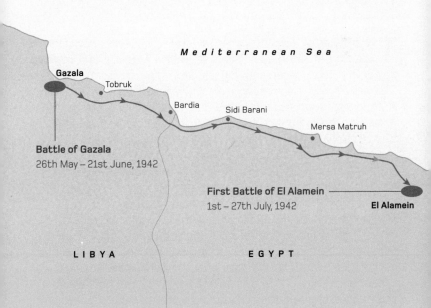

Rommel's second offensive

Mediterranean Sea

Gazala

Tobruk

Bardia

Sidi Barani

Mersa Matruh

Battle of Gazala
26th May – 21st June, 1942

First Battle of El Alamein
1st – 27th July, 1942

El Alamein

LIBYA

EGYPT

Britain's Middle East interventions

The oilfields of Iraq and Iran were vital to the Allied war effort. In April 1941 an Arab nationalist, Rashid Ali al-Gaylani, took power in a coup in Iraq and appealed for support from the Germans. The British responded with a small but decisive military intervention that swiftly ousted Rashid Ali and installed a pro-British government. In the case of Iran, the country's ruler Reza Shah Pahlavi was suspected of pro-German sympathies. Britain and the Soviet Union cooperated in an invasion with substantial forces in August 1941. The Iranian army was easily overcome and the shah forced to abdicate. His son Mohammed Reza Pahlavi took the throne he would hold until 1979. In the eastern Mediterranean Britain and France were rival colonial powers. The British controlled Palestine while the French ran neighbouring Syria and Lebanon. In June 1941, fearing that the Vichy French authorities might provide bases for the Luftwaffe, British and Free French troops mounted an invasion of Syria from Palestine and Iraq. After some sharp fighting the country was secured and the Free French replaced the Vichy administration.

The Emir Abdulla of Transjordan rides with Australian troops during the Syria campaign.

Joseph Stalin

Soviet dictator Joseph Stalin was born Joseph Vissarionovich Djugashvili, son of a Georgian shoemaker. He made his name as one of the leaders of the Bolshevik Revolution in Russia in 1917. By the 1930s he had made himself the all-powerful ruler of the Soviet Union, the world's first communist state. His rule was characterized by ruthless brutality and paranoia. Responsibility for millions of deaths lay at his door. Yet Stalin continued to command widespread admiration on the left as the leader of a workers' state and a future world revolution.

Stalin's cynical deal with Hitler in August 1939 showed his single-minded dedication to preserving the Soviet state. He saw no reason to aid the capitalist Western democracies or right-wing Poland. He knew a future war with Nazi Germany was possible, even probable, but in summer 1941 refused to listen to warnings of an imminent German attack. This folly certainly contributed to his country's early defeats in the war, but Stalin would later provide formidable willpower to drive the defence of the Soviet Union.

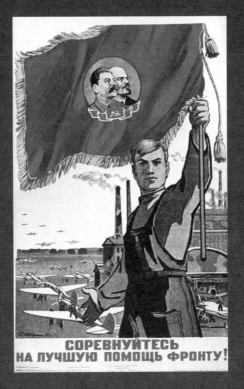

СОРЕВНУЙТЕСЬ
НА ЛУЧШУЮ ПОМОЩЬ ФРОНТУ!

'Follow This Worker's Example and Produce
More For The Front'. Russian poster 1942.

The Katyn Massacre

In 1939, as part of its deal with Nazi Germany, the Soviet Union annexed eastern Poland. The Soviet secret police, the NKVD, embarked upon a campaign of mass arrests and killings of Polish priests, landowners and the educated elite. The Soviets had also taken at least 250,000 Polish prisoners of war. In March 1940 Stalin approved an NKVD plan for the mass execution of captured Polish officers. Through April and May almost 8,000 officers and some 14,000 other Poles were executed at the Katyn Forest near Smolensk and several other sites. The victims were shot in the back of the head and buried in mass graves.

In April 1943, when invading German forces were in occupation of Smolensk, the Nazis publicized the existence of the Katyn killing fields. Their intention was to break up the alliance between the Soviet Union and the Western democracies by the revelation of this atrocity. The Soviets denied responsibility until the 1990s. The Katyn Massacre constituted only a small percentage of the total killings carried out by the NKVD during World War II.

A memorial to the Katyn Massacre, Katyn Forest, Poland.

Soviet occupations

In June 1940 half a million Red Army soldiers marched into the Baltic states of Estonia, Latvia and Lithuania, which were absorbed into the Soviet Union. Two weeks later Soviet threats forced Romania to hand over the border areas of Bessarabia and part of Bukovina. Soviet occupation was followed by the usual Stalinist horrors of mass killing of 'class enemies' and deportations. Along with the occupation of eastern Poland in 1939, these gains expanded Soviet territory by over 400,000 sq km (155,000 sq mi). This Soviet expansion was broadly in line with the treaty made with Nazi Germany in August 1939, but Hitler was not pleased to see Soviet forces advance so far westward. Although Stalin fulfilled his obligations to supply his Nazi ally with food and fuel, by autumn 1940 tension between Germany and the Soviet Union was palpable. Soviet arms production was stepped up and the Red Army war-gamed resistance to a German invasion. Work progressed on construction of a fortified line along the Soviet Union's new western border, but progress was too slow. The defences would be incomplete when Hitler struck.

Soviet troops arrive in the Latvian capital of Riga, 1940.

Hitler plans to conquer the East

As early as August 1940, Hitler informed his generals of his intention 'to smash the Soviet state in one blow'. He would have preferred to defeat Britain before striking eastward, but now envisaged that the defeat of the Soviet Union would remove Britain's last hope. Beyond these strategic considerations lay Hitler's long-term vision of a racially stratified future. He intended to colonize all of Ukraine and European Russia, reducing the Slav population to servile status under the control of German settlers. His objective was also ideological – the destruction of the only communist state. On 18th December 1940 Hitler signed a war directive ordering preparation for Operation Barbarossa, the invasion of the Soviet Union. A target date was set for the following May, although this eventually slipped to late June, largely because of the unexpected spring operation against Yugoslavia and Greece. Hitler was clear about the nature of the campaign to be waged in the Soviet Union. On 30th March 1941 he told his generals the normal rules of war would not apply: 'This is a war of annihilation'.

The title page of Hitler's life story,
Mein Kampf (*My Struggle*), in which
he claimed Germany had a right to seize
cultivatable land in Russia.

Operation Barbarossa launched

To attack the Soviet Union Hitler assembled the largest invasion force ever seen, around 3.8 million men with 3,500 tanks and over 2,000 aircraft. The troops were mainly German, aided by substantial Finnish and Romanian forces and smaller contingents from other Axis countries. Launched on 22nd June 1941 the offensive overwhelmed poorly organized Soviet defences. More than a thousand Soviet aircraft were destroyed within hours, surprised on the ground by Luftwaffe attacks on air bases. Red Army soldiers, exposed in forward positions, were bewildered by the speed of enemy action and cut off. Hastily mounted, incoherent Soviet counter-attacks sacrificed lives to no effect. As Axis forces pushed deep into Soviet territory, Stalin at first seemed paralyzed. On 3rd July, however, he made a radio broadcast to the Soviet people. Evoking traditional Russian patriotism, he called for popular resistance to the invader and a scorched-earth policy to deny advancing enemy forces food and fuel. Severe police measures were instituted against 'whimperers and cowards' among the Soviet population. A titanic struggle had begun.

German troops in Russia. The onslaught against the Soviets took place along a 2,900-km-long (1,800-mile) front.

Soviets overwhelmed

The Axis forces committed to Barbarossa were divided into three groups. Army Group North thrust through the Baltic states towards Leningrad (St Petersburg); Army Group Centre, the most powerful formation, headed for Minsk, with beyond that Smolensk and Moscow; and Army Group South attacked Ukraine, striking towards Kiev. Hitler's objective was to destroy Soviet forces through a series of enveloping manoeuvres that would trap them in 'pockets'. An encirclement at Minsk in late June netted 280,000 prisoners. In mid-July some 300,000 Soviet troops were captured at Smolensk, and as many as half a million may have surrendered in the Kiev pocket in mid-September. Few of the Soviet prisoners were to survive captivity. Despite these major defeats, the Red Army was able to draft in fresh troops and keep fighting. The Germans, meanwhile, had lost half a million men dead or wounded in the first two months' fighting. Focusing on the Ukraine and the northern front, Hitler did not prioritize a drive to capture Moscow until September. This was to prove too late in the year.

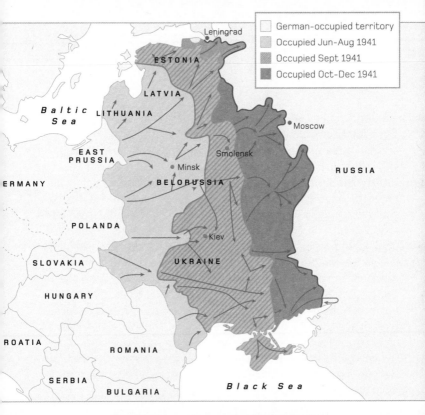

The German advance in the East, 1941

The Siege of Leningrad

In September 1941 Leningrad was surrounded by Finnish troops advancing from the north and Germans from the south. Faced with the prospect of heavy losses overcoming the city's defences, vigorously organized by General Georgi Zhukov, Hitler preferred to settle for a siege. While placing Leningrad under artillery and air bombardment, the Germans set out to starve the population to death. Some three million people were trapped with no access to food supplies. Dogs and cats were cooked and wallpaper paste was used to make bread. Through the winter of 1941–42 hundreds of thousands died. A road was built across the winter ice of Lake Ladoga to reach the railhead at Tikhvin and gradually the supply situation improved, but through 1942 a series of Soviet counter-offensives failed to liberate the city. In January 1943 a land corridor was opened up through German lines, linking Leningrad to Soviet territory, yet the bombardment continued for another year. By the time German forces were finally driven off, after a siege lasting 872 days, a total of around 1.2 million people had died.

An artillery shell explodes in Leningrad, September 1941.

Nazi massacres after Barbarossa

Because of the brutality of Soviet rule, in 1941 many people in Ukraine and the Baltic states welcomed the Germans as liberators. They were soon disillusioned. Before Barbarossa, German bureaucrats had drawn up a 'Hunger Plan', suggesting that 30 million Soviet citizens would need to die, by starvation or massacre, to free up food from Russia and Ukraine for German consumption. The commissar order, issued to members of the German army before the invasion, directed that all communist officials were to be killed out of hand.

The SS organized paramilitary death squads, called *Einsatzgruppen*, to follow behind the advancing German armies. Their mission included the mass killing of Jews, who lived in large numbers in the western Soviet Union. At Kiev on 29th–30th September 1941, some 33,000 Jews were killed by SS paramilitaries and Ukrainian collaborators – machine-gunned and their bodies buried in the ravine at Babi Yar. There were similar massacres from the Baltic states to Crimea.

The execution of Russian Jews. It is estimated that the *Einsatzgruppen* killed two million people during the war in Poland and the Soviet Union, more than half of them Jewish.

The Soviet defence of Moscow

In October 1941 Hitler announced that the Soviet Union was beaten and 'would never rise again'. Axis forces advancing towards Moscow destroyed more Soviet armies at Vyazma and Bryansk. In the Soviet capital panic reigned as people fled the city. But Stalin stayed in Moscow, the NKVD ruthlessly restored order and Zhukov took over the task of organizing the city's defences. For the Germans, difficulties accumulated. Their supply system, reliant on horse-drawn wagons, broke down when autumn rains made roads impassable. The rain was followed by savagely cold weather, for which German troops were ill prepared. The Soviets meanwhile transferred fresh troops from Manchuria. By early December the Germans had reached the outskirts of Moscow, but were suffering from frostbite and much of their equipment would not function in the extreme cold. On 5th December Zhukov launched a counter-offensive, using shock troops to penetrate the German lines. The Germans were forced to withdraw to avoid encirclement. Furious, Hitler sacked all his army group commanders. His gamble on a swift victory in the East had failed.

ОТСТОИМ МОСКВУ!

'Make a stand for Moscow!'

The Red Army

The Soviet Red Army was a fighting force that ran on fear. Every army commander was shadowed by a political commissar and the NKVD secret police were omnipresent. Even in the thick of battle officers and men were arrested or executed for criticizing Stalin. Any soldier who surrendered was denounced as a traitor. Punishment battalions led attacks, marched through enemy minefields with NKVD pistols pointed at their backs. About 160,000 Soviet soldiers were executed during the war. As Stalin once said: 'It takes a brave man to be a coward in the Red Army'.

Yet from commanding officers to ordinary conscripts, the Red Army fought with courage and tenacity, motivated above all by outrage at the destruction Axis forces visited upon their country. Soviet industry, relocated out of enemy range beyond the Urals, provided the tools for the job – notably the T-34 tank with a powerful gun, good armour and reliability that made it among the war's most effective weapons. About one in three of the 34 million Soviet soldiers who fought in the war lost their lives.

Soldiers of the Red Army parade in Red Square, Moscow, before launching a counter-offensive against the Germans, 7th November 1941.

An uneasy alliance

On the same day that Hitler launched Operation Barbarossa, Winston Churchill declared Britain's solidarity with the Soviet Union. A formal military alliance followed three weeks later. Churchill was a virulent anti-communist, but hostility to Hitler outweighed all other considerations. Stalin's attitude to the Western democracies was similar. He did not trust them at all, but wartime expediency dictated the need for cooperation.

In August 1941 the United States extended Lend-Lease, its arrangement for supplying arms to Britain, to include the Soviet Union. Stalin was soon complaining about the quantity of equipment the Western powers were sending and their failure to open a 'second front' through an invasion of occupied Europe. When Churchill met Stalin in Moscow in August 1942, only a shared taste for heavy drinking rescued their rapport. The first summit meeting of the 'Big Three', Roosevelt, Churchill and Stalin, at Teheran in 1943, confirmed the Grand Alliance while skating over future differences.

British Prime Minister
Winston Churchill meets
Soviet premiere Joseph
Stalin at the Moscow
Conference in August 1942.

The Arctic convoys

From September 1941, Britain and the United States sent military supplies to the Soviet Union through the Arctic ports of Arkhangelsk and Murmansk. Sailing around the north of German-occupied Norway, merchant convoys not only faced awful weather conditions – ice, fog, gales and freezing temperatures – but also were exposed to attack by land-based Luftwaffe aircraft, U-boats and surface warships lurking in the Norwegian fjords.

The Allies suffered a disaster in summer 1942, when convoy PQ-17, formed of 35 merchant ships, was ordered to scatter and proceed unescorted due to a mistaken belief it was about to be attacked by German surface warships. Twenty-two of the defenceless merchantmen were sunk by air and submarine attack. The Allies also scored successes, however, notably in December 1943, when the German battle cruiser *Scharnhorst*, sortieing from its Norwegian base to attack a convoy, was sunk by an escort force including the battleship *Duke of York*.

ARMS FOR RUSSIA . . . A great convoy of British ships escorted by Soviet fighter planes sails into Murmansk harbour with vital supplies for the Red Army.

n the course of the war, the Arctic convoys delivered almost four million tonnes of war material to the Soviet Union, including 5,000 tanks and 7,000 aircraft

Germany's eastern advance continues

The counter-offensive launched by the Soviet forces in December 1941 had come to a halt by March 1942. Although the Germans had been forced back, they retained key strongpoints such as Vyazma, Khursk and Kharkov. When Stalin tried to resume the offensive at Kharkov in May, the Red Army suffered massive losses to a well-coordinated German counter-attack. Meanwhile, Hitler had been planning his own resumed offensive. Concentrating his forces in the south, he ordered a drive towards the strategically vital Baku oilfields in the Caucasus, between the Caspian and the Black seas. Launched in late June, the southern offensive was overwhelmingly successful. Flooding forward to the Don River, by August Axis forces had cut the oil pipeline from the Caucasus at Rostov. The fall of the Soviet port of Sebastopol in July left the whole of Crimea in German hands. As well as capturing the oilfields, however, Hitler wanted to take the city of Stalingrad on the Volga. He divided his forces, sending German 6th Army to Stalingrad. This was a fateful decision that would lead to disaster.

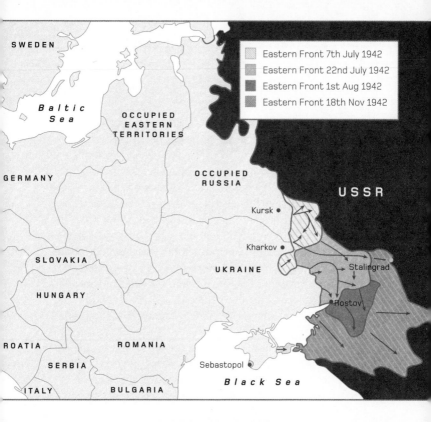

Eastern Front, 1942

The Nazi New Order

The victories of 1939–41 gave Nazi Germany domination over a vast area of Europe. Many people assumed this would be a permanent state of affairs. German technocrats floated plans for a 'New Order' – a European state dominated by Germany, with the Reichsmark as the single currency. Hitler, however, envisaged the future in terms of a brutal racial hierarchy, with Germanic Aryans pitilessly exploiting Slavs in eastern lands ruled as a colonial empire, and with no place for Jews at all. In practice, Germany's aim was to plunder the maximum of money, goods, labour and food from conquered countries, and systems of rule were improvised for this purpose. The Netherlands, for example, was placed under a civilian commissioner, while Belgium had a military commander. In such countries, the existing civil service and police continued to function under German orders. In contrast, Slav countries such as Poland, Ukraine and Russia were subjected to lawless German oppression designed to eradicate all trace of nationhood and reduce the population to servile status.

	Germany/German-occupied
	Germany's allies
	Allies
	Neutral

Iceland

Norway

Sweden

Finland

SOVIET
UNION

Ireland

Great
Britain

Denmark

The
Netherlands

Belgium

Greater
Germany

Occupied
France

Bohemia/Moravia

Slovakia

Switz.

Hungary

Vichy
France

Italy

Croatia

Serbia

Romania

Bulgaria

Spain

Corsica

Balearic
Islands

Sardinia

Turkey

Sicily

Greece

Cyprus

Crete

Europe in 1942

Pro-Nazi collaboration

In the countries of Nazi-occupied Europe, most people continued their daily lives, which in practice meant broadly collaborating with the German occupiers. Some individuals and movements, such as the Croatian nationalist Ustase organization, saw a more positive opportunity in Axis victory. After the defeat of Yugoslavia in 1941, Italy and Germany allowed Ustase leader Ante Pavelic to lead a Croat puppet state, whose militia carried out brutal atrocities against Serbs, Jews and Roma, killing possibly half a million people. The Nazis also found collaborators in mass murder in the Baltic states and Ukraine. Hitler was ambivalent towards collaborators. For example, Norwegian fascist politician Vidkun Quisling, prime minister for some of the war, acted as an ally of Germany but was not allowed any real power.

Substantial numbers of foreign volunteers were recruited into the Waffen SS – 40,000 from Belgium, 25,000 from the Netherlands and 6,000 from Denmark. Enthusiasm for collaboration declined sharply once it became evident Germany was losing the war.

FOR DANMARK!
MOD BOLCHEVISMEN!

This Danish pro-Nazi propaganda poster reads: 'For Denmark! Against Bolshevism!'

Vichy France

The French regime, established at Vichy under Marshal Philippe Pétain in 1940, willingly collaborated with Nazi Germany. Blaming defeat on the lax and pleasure-loving Third Republic, Vichy leaders tried to build a paternalist conservative France, with measures ranging from limits on alcohol to subsidies for larger families. They also introduced their own anti-Semitic laws. Despite the efforts of the pro-German Pierre Laval, however, Vichy France did not become an ally of Germany in its war against Britain, a meeting between Pétain and Hitler at Montroie in October 1940 producing no result. France's aspirations to regain status as a European power depended on its extensive empire, which remained loyal to Vichy. Syria was lost to the British and Free French in July 1941, and in November 1942 the Allies invaded French North Africa. The Germans reacted to the invasion by sending troops to occupy the Vichy-controlled zone, although they failed to capture the French fleet at Toulon, which was scuttled before they arrived. From the end of 1942 the Vichy regime, without French territory or an empire to rule, became largely an irrelevance.

Members of the legion of veterans stand with a poster of 84-year-old Marshal Pétain, Vichy France, 1941.

The French resistance

In June 1940 an overwhelming majority of French people accepted defeat and, in the zone of France occupied by the Germans, at least passively collaborated with the occupiers. The first small resistance groups emerged in late 1940, chiefly engaged in the dissemination of underground newspapers. After the Nazi invasion of the Soviet Union in June 1941, the French Communist Party, which until then supported the Nazi-Soviet Pact, switched to opposing the occupation. Used to covert action and tight discipline, communist groups launched a campaign of sabotage and assassination of German officers from August 1941. The Nazis responded with mass executions. De Gaulle's Free French movement in London was eager to unify and lead the emerging resistance. In January 1942 Jean Moulin was parachuted into France to fulfil this task. Political divisions between rival resistance groups were acute and it was not until May 1943 that Moulin was able to persuade the eight largest movements to found the National Council of Resistance in Paris. Moulin was betrayed to the Gestapo the following month and died in captivity.

Life goes on at the Café de la Paix, Paris, with high-ranking officers and soldiers of the German Wehrmacht sitting among the local patrons.

The Free French

After General de Gaulle's appeal for France to continue fighting, delivered on 18th June 1940, only some 7,000 troops rallied to him in London and, among the French colonies, only French Equatorial Africa and Pacific island territories. The first military operations by the Free French forces, in association with the British, were against the Vichy French – notably an unsuccessful raid on Dakar in French West Africa in September 1940 and the capture of Syria in July 1941. In May to June 1942 General Marie Pierre Koenig's First French Infantry Brigade, comprising Foreign Legionnaires and troops from Equatorial Africa and the Pacific territories, distinguished themselves fighting as part of British Eighth Army at Bir Hakeim in the Desert War. The scale of the Free French forces expanded massively when joined by previously Vichy troops from North Africa in late 1942. They fought as an expeditionary force in Italy the following year and later in the liberation of France. Free French forces remained in the majority colonial troops, including Moroccans, Algerians and Senegalese, and Foreign Legionnaires – ironically, many of them German.

Brigadier General Charles de Gaulle reviews French navy
sailors willing to pursue the fight as Free French Forces.

General de Gaulle

At the time of France's defeat several senior politicians and generals favoured continuing the fight from abroad, but it was the little-known General Charles de Gaulle who succeeded in reaching London and launching the call to arms on 18th June 1940. De Gaulle had fought in World War I and later became an advocate of mobile armoured warfare. He had commanded an armoured division in May 1940 before entering the government as undersecretary for war. De Gaulle possessed none of the fame or status of World War I hero Pétain, but through radio broadcasts he exercised a mounting influence inside France. His allies, especially the Americans, found his prickly French patriotism insufferable, but although several attempts were made to find an alternative French leader, de Gaulle outmanoeuvred all his rivals. Acknowledged as the leader both of Free French forces outside France and of the French Resistance, he developed a detailed plan to take control of France after liberation. As a result, in 1944 he was able to form a provisional government and begin re-establishing France's status as a great power.

General de Gaulle, making his London broadcast of 18th June 1940.

Poles in exile

During the war, London was home to governments-in-exile from a number of Nazi-occupied countries, including Norway, Belgium, the Netherlands, Czechoslovakia and Poland. Of these the Poles had by far the greatest military significance. Tens of thousands of Polish military personnel escaped to the West in 1939, many serving in the Battle of France before reassembling in Britain under their prime minister and commander-in-chief, General Władysław Sikorski. From 1942, Polish forces were augmented by 80,000 prisoners of war released from captivity in the Soviet Union and reaching the West via Iran. Polish armed forces in the West eventually numbered almost 200,000, playing an especially notable role in the Italian campaign. In April 1943 the revelation of the Katyn Massacre fouled relations between the Polish exiles and the Soviet Union. The government-in-exile's resistance movement, the Polish Home Army, was decimated in the Warsaw uprising in 1944 (see page 330). Most of the Polish soldiers in the West stayed in exile, never returning to communist-ruled postwar Poland.

Władysław Sikorski. When he died in an air crash in Gibraltar in 1943, there were rumours Stalin's agents had assassinated him.

Neutrality

Neutrality did not save the Netherlands, Belgium, Denmark or Norway from invasion, but Sweden and Switzerland remained free of occupation through partial collaboration with the Nazis, the Swedes providing Germany with iron ore and the Swiss with banking facilities. The neutrality of the Republic of Ireland reflected the anti-British sentiments of the Taoiseach Eamon de Valera and of many other Irish people. Despite official neutrality, some 70,000 men from the republic individually volunteered to serve in the British armed forces during the war.

The most surprising neutrality was that of Franco's Spain. Since Franco had won the Spanish Civil War with German and Italian aid, he was expected to join the Axis. However, when Franco met Hitler on the Spanish-French border at Hendaye in October 1940, they could not agree on terms for Spain to enter the war. Spanish neutrality blocked Axis plans to seize the British base at Gibraltar. Nonetheless, in 1941 Franco sent 20,000 Blue Division volunteers to fight for Hitler against the Soviet Union.

Hitler and Eberhard von Stohrer (centre) meet Franco at Hendaye.

Himmler's SS

Originally organized as Hitler's personal guard, the *Schutzstaffel* (SS) grew to become one of the most important elements in the Nazi state and the armed forces. The *Allgemeine SS* (General SS) was a paramilitary police force that implemented Nazi racial and political policies through a reign of terror. The *Waffen SS* (Armed SS) provided more than 30 divisions of troops by the end of the war, including armoured formations, fighting on all major fronts. The SS also ran the Nazi system of concentration camps and death camps, an operation that became a substantial business enterprise exploiting slave labour. By 1945 the SS numbered around one million men. The leader of the SS was Heinrich Himmler, a Nazi Party member from 1923. Himmler was especially devoted to racial ideology. He encouraged Dutch, Flemish and Scandinavian volunteers to join the SS because they were of appropriate 'Aryan' stock. The SS ran the *Lebensborn* programme that, among other measures, abducted 'Aryan-looking' children from their parents in Slav countries to be raised in Germany.

Heinrich Himmler visits a prisoner-of-war camp. He committed suicide in May 1945, after being taken as a prisoner of war himself.

The Nazi camps

The first German concentration camp was opened at Dachau in March 1933, less than two months after Hitler became chancellor. Those imprisoned were initially the Nazis' political opponents, the communists and socialists. After the outbreak of war the camp system expanded massively, filling with Jews, homosexuals, Roma and other 'undesirables'. Resistance fighters from occupied countries and Soviet prisoners of war were held there, too. Slave labour was vital to the German war economy. The death toll in the concentration camps was high – through overwork, mistreatment, malnutrition and random execution.

From 1941 the Nazis also created death camps, mostly located in German-occupied Poland. Prisoners were brought to these camps simply to be killed, most exterminated within a few hours of arrival. Of these, Auschwitz and Majdanek also served as concentration camps providing factory labour, so they had thousands of survivors. At Belzec, a pure extermination camp, only seven of the half million people transported there survived.

Shoes belonging to prisoners at Majdanek, one of several camps in Poland that also included Sobibor, Belzec, Chelmno, Treblinka and Auschwitz.

The yellow star

Nazi persecution of the Jews, begun in Greater Germany before 1939, was given far larger scope once World War II was underway. The conquest of Poland placed around three million Jews in Nazi hands, and the German victories of 1940–41 added further millions. Nazi policy was to segregate the Jews, either by physically removing them to ghettoes, as was done in Poland, or at least identifying them with a compulsory mark. From 1941 this mark was usually a yellow Star of David with the word 'Jew' written on it in the local language.

The Nazis' long-term aim was to rid Europe completely of its Jewish population. In 1940 a plan was floated to deport all Jews to the French African colony of Madagascar, but nothing came of this. The extermination of Jews began in piecemeal fashion, driven by Himmler's SS, who in 1941 authorized mass killings of Jewish people in conquered areas of the Soviet Union and in Poland. The organized drive for a Europe-wide 'Final Solution' began in 1942.

The Final Solution

The Wannsee Conference, a polite gathering held in Berlin in January 1942, secured the cooperation of German civil servants and diplomats for an SS-run programme to exterminate the European Jews. Across the continent, Jewish men, women and children were to be rounded up and deported by train to Nazi-administered Poland, where camps with gas chambers were being built to carry out murder on an industrial scale. The trains began to run in spring 1942, carrying first Jews from the Polish ghettoes and Germany, then from France, Belgium, Norway and the Netherlands. As many as three million were killed in the first year. Many more followed – the Jews of Greece and Italy in 1943, the Hungarian Jews in spring 1944. The Holocaust was financed by stolen Jewish money, but it still diverted resources from the German war effort. The best chance for Jews lay in the German need for slave labour, which motivated the Nazis to keep some of the able-bodied alive. In a war full of atrocities, the Holocaust stood out for its scale, irrationality and sheer cold-blooded awfulness.

Villa Marlier, site of the 1942 Wannsee Conference, Berlin.

The Warsaw ghetto uprising

The Warsaw ghetto uprising was the war's largest armed revolt by victims of the Holocaust. The Nazis had driven 400,000 Polish Jews into the small area of the ghetto by autumn 1940, enclosed behind a wall and barbed wire. Grossly overcrowded and starved of food, thousands died. In summer 1942, the SS began the mass deportation of ghetto inhabitants to the Treblinka extermination camp. Some 250,000 died there. Officially the deportations were a 'resettlement' in work camps, but the truth became known in the ghetto. Facing certain death, Jewish groups organized armed resistance, obtaining a limited range of weaponry. On 18th January 1943 they rebuffed a German attempt to resume the deportations. Full-scale German retaliation began on 19th April. Some 2,000 heavily armed Waffen SS troops entered the ghetto, destroying it building by building. Around 150 Germans and perhaps 7,000 Jews were killed in fighting that ended with the destruction of the Warsaw Great Synagogue on 16th May 1943. All surviving Jews from the ghetto, around 50,000 people, were transported to death camps and exterminated.

German soldiers take prisoners during the
destruction of the Warsaw ghetto, Poland, 1943.

Auschwitz

The largest and most infamous of the Nazi wartime camps was Auschwitz in southern Poland. It was originally created in 1940 as a concentration camp for Poles. In 1941 a second camp was built, Auschwitz-Birkenau, as an extermination centre where Jews and others were killed in gas chambers using the pesticide Zyklon B. A third large camp, Auschwitz-Monowitz, provided labour for a factory manufacturing synthetic rubber. When Jews arrived at Auschwitz by train, those deemed unsuitable for work were immediately taken to the gas chambers. Those selected to work had no great chance of long-term survival – the average life expectancy of factory workers was three months.

The Allies learned of the existence of Auschwitz from reports by the Polish Home Army resistance movement and escaped Jewish prisoners. Plans to bomb the site or the railway leading to it, although discussed, never materialized. No precise figure can be given for the number of people killed at Auschwitz, but estimates suggest around 1.5 million died there, 90 per cent of them Jews.

The gates at Auschwitz, above which runs the Nazi motto 'work sets you free'.

Allied POWs in Europe

Some 200,000 British and almost 100,000 American servicemen were captured by German and Italian forces in the course of World War II, along with almost two million French and up to five million Soviet troops. Soviet prisoners were grossly mistreated, more than half dying in captivity, but the captured servicemen of the Western Allies generally enjoyed the protection of the Geneva Convention. They were allowed to receive food parcels through the International Red Cross and to exchange letters with their families. Officers were exempted from work, as the convention dictated, though other ranks were forced to labour under guard in factories or on farms. The German POW camps were run by the army, not the SS. Many ingenious escape schemes were devised by POWs. French prisoners had the best chance of a 'home run' because it was so much easier to reach France than Britain. Escape attempts could bring down severe punishment. In the case of the famous 'Great Escape' from Stalag Luft III in March 1944, 50 of the 73 recaptured escapees were summarily executed by the SS.

An identity tag worn by a prisoner of war at
Stalag VII/A, Moosburg, Germany, 1943–44.

Colditz

Before the Nazi era the medieval castle at Colditz in Saxony, southern Germany, had been used to house the insane. In 1939 it became Oflag IV-C, an especially high-security POW facility for housing captured Allied officers who had made attempts to escape from other camps. Deemed escape-proof, Colditz proved anything but, and it became a point of honour for officers to escape if they possibly could.

There were more guards than prisoners assigned to the castle, but the regime there was surprisingly lax. The POWs were free to roam the building, whose complex passageways and time-worn tunnels offered much potential for concealment. On one occasion a glider was built inside Colditz without the guards noticing. On the other hand, punishments for breach of rules could be severe, one POW enduring a total of more than a year in solitary confinement. Thirty-one Allied prisoners made successful escapes from Colditz, most of them crossing the border into neutral Switzerland. The camp was liberated by US forces in April 1945.

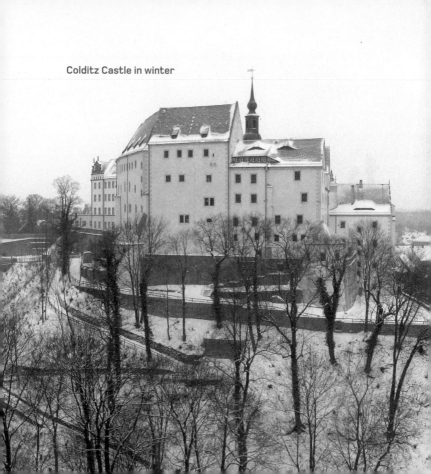

Colditz Castle in winter

American neutrality eroded

As Europe slid into war in 1939, popular sentiment in the United States was isolationist. It was widely felt that America had been wrong to be drawn into involvement in World War I and should not repeat the mistake. In the 1930s Congress had passed a series of Neutrality Acts, designed to make it legally impossible for a president to embroil the country in foreign conflicts. On 3rd September 1939 President Franklin D Roosevelt duly promised the American people that 'the nation will remain a neutral nation'. Yet the president feared the rise of Nazi Germany. In November he succeeded in having the neutrality legislation revised to allow the supply of arms to Britain and France on a 'cash-and-carry' basis. In September 1940 Roosevelt agreed to give Britain 50 old US destroyers in return for bases in British territories, a move severely criticized by isolationists. Fighting that year's presidential election, Roosevelt felt bound to renew his promise 'to keep our people out of foreign wars', but American factories were already the main suppliers keeping Britain in the fight.

Prosperity and normality reign on US city streets in 1940.

President Franklin D Roosevelt

Hailing from a prominent Dutch-American family, Roosevelt served as Assistant Secretary of the Navy during World War I. Despite being crippled by polio in 1921, he won the 1932 presidential election and gained popularity through his New Deal programme to counter the Great Depression. Controversially ignoring the convention that presidents serve no more than two terms, he won re-election three times. He was convinced by 1939 that the expanding power of Nazi Germany posed a threat to American security. He also viewed the rise of militarism in Japan with concern. His preference was to keep America out of actual fighting and he hesitated to commit the country to a war without the full backing of the American people. The Japanese attack on Pearl Harbor (see page 206) and subsequent German declaration of war on America resolved this problem. Roosevelt did not take as direct control of military matters as did Stalin, Hitler and Churchill. Critics have argued he was naive about Stalin's intentions and that ill-health undermined his judgment later in the war. Roosevelt died weeks before victory over Germany in April 1945.

The arsenal of democracy

Victory in the presidential election of November 1940 freed Roosevelt to pursue a more active policy of support for Britain. Fulfilling British war orders had decisively refloated the American economy, creating many thousands of jobs that were in effect dependent upon a pro-British policy. American sentiment had also been turned in favour of the British through the gallant spectacle of the Battle of Britain and the Blitz. On 29th December 1940 Roosevelt delivered a radio broadcast in which he warned that America could not be safe if Axis powers controlled the other continents and called for the country to act as 'the great arsenal of democracy'. A block to implementation of this policy was Britain's dwindling financial strength, which left it unable to pay for American-produced war material. In March 1941 the Lend-Lease programme was initiated, under which the United States supplied military equipment, food and fuel without payment, initially to Britain and China, and subsequently also to the Soviet Union. Lend-Lease effectively ended any pretence of American neutrality, without yet committing US forces to a shooting war.

American twin-engine bombers provided under the Lend-Lease programme are hoisted aboard ship for transportation.

America gears up for war

In 1939 the United States was unprepared for a major conflict. Its only military claim to great power status lay in the battleships and carriers of the US navy. The country had a smaller army than Poland or Romania and its Army Air Corps was equally starved of funds. The country's first peacetime conscription was introduced in September 1940. Under the leadership of Chief of Staff General George Marshall, the US army embarked upon an accelerated expansion that was to see its troop numbers increase fortyfold in three years.

The first clashes between US and German forces occurred at sea without a declaration of war. From July 1941 America assumed responsibility for the defence of merchant convoys west of Iceland, an area occupied by US forces. On 4th September a US destroyer on escort duty carried out a depth-charge attack on a German U-boat. After a number of other incidents, on 31st October, the destroyer USS *Reuben James* was sunk by a U-boat with the loss of a hundred lives. This was war in all but name.

Man the
GUNS
Join the NAVY

The Atlantic Charter

In 1941 the British were desperate to overcome Roosevelt's caution and draw America into the war. British and American military chiefs held talks in January and March about cooperation in the event of the United States joining the war, but discussions remained hypothetical. In August 1941 Churchill and Roosevelt travelled to Placentia Bay, Newfoundland, for their first face-to-face meeting, the prime minister on board the battleship *Prince of Wales* and the president on the heavy cruiser *Augusta*. Churchill was disappointed to find the president still unready to fight, but the meeting did produce a declaration that was in effect a joint statement of war aims. Dubbed by journalists the 'Atlantic Charter', it declared that Britain and the United States desired no territorial gains and committed them to the principles of self-determination (glossing over Britain's African and Asian colonies), free trade and international economic cooperation. A future peace would be based on disarmament and a global 'system of general security'. The Atlantic Charter would later evolve into the principles of the United Nations.

The historic meeting between Winston Churchill and
Franklin D Roosevelt aboard HMS *Prince of Wales*, 1941.

America enters the European war

The Japanese attack on Pearl Harbor on 7th December 1941 was welcomed as good news not only by Churchill, who wanted America in the war, but also by Hitler. The Führer had long considered war with America inevitable. Now the United States and Britain would have to divert resources to fight the Japanese, putting Nazi Germany in a far stronger position. On 11th December Hitler declared war on the United States, denouncing Roosevelt as 'mentally unsound' and an agent of the world Jewish conspiracy against Germany. The American people sought revenge against Japan, but Hitler's declaration of war allowed Roosevelt to follow his preferred strategy, prioritizing the war in Europe. From 22nd December US and British leaders met in Washington for the Arcadia Conference. Building on their discussions over the previous year, they created a unified military command, the Combined Chiefs of Staff, establishing the basis for what General Marshall called 'the most complete unification of military effort ever achieved by two allied nations'. The Americans committed themselves to regarding Germany as 'the prime enemy'.

US troops drive through London, England, 1942.

U-boats in American waters

An immediate consequence of the outbreak of war between the United States and the Axis powers was an upturn in the German U-boat campaign. Even before the formal declaration of war, U-boat chief Admiral Karl Dönitz had developed plans to send long-range Type IX submarines into US coastal waters. From January 1942, U-boats ranged from Newfoundland down to the Gulf of Mexico. There was no blackout in America, nor had the US navy organized a convoy system for merchant ships. The U-boats feasted upon isolated targets silhouetted against shore lights, at first meeting almost no opposition. Torpedoed oil tankers blazing off shore became a familiar spectacle for coastal dwellers. Mid-ocean refuelling from submarine tankers, known as 'milk cows', allowed the U-boats to stay in the western Atlantic for long periods. Shipping sunk by U-boats rose from 124,000 tonnes in December 1941 to 700,000 tonnes in June 1942, mostly attributed to sinkings in US coastal waters. The carnage eventually subsided, through the belated introduction of a convoy system and submarine-spotting patrols by radar-equipped aircraft.

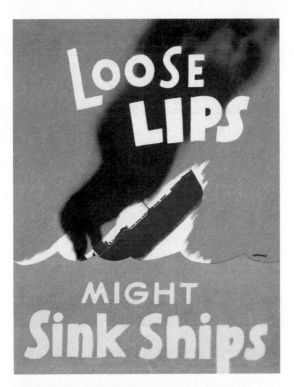

An American propaganda poster warns servicemen and civilians that careless talk could compromise the war effort.

The US wartime economy

The phenomenal expansion of production in the United States during the war was one of the keys to victory. In the course of the war American factories built more than 300,000 aircraft, over 100 aircraft carriers, 80,000 landing craft and 100,000 armoured vehicles. The United States had ready access to raw materials and a large workforce undisturbed by enemy attack, but this rapid expansion was also a tribute to American organizational ability. Smooth cooperation between federal government, the military and private corporations ensured the forces mostly received weapons appropriate to their needs. Intelligent decision-making was essential, as in the adoption of simplified designs suited to mass production – cargo vessels known as Liberty ships, for example, were assembled from prefabricated parts. Americans profited from the war. Many found steady jobs in federal administration, which grew from one million to four million employees. Farm incomes doubled as small hard-scrabble farms of the 'dust bowl' era were supplanted by large-scale agriculture. In wartime production lay the basis for postwar prosperity.

The production line of a Western aircraft plant at Fort Worth, Texas.

Rosie the Riveter

Among the most famous symbols of wartime life in the US was 'Rosie the Riveter', the idealized type of tough American woman engaged in essential war work. Labour shortages created by the departure of men to the forces and the expansion of war industries made a drive to employ more women unavoidable. The number of women in employment increased by five million during the war, making up one-third of the total workforce by 1945. Especially striking was the scale of women's work in heavy industry with, for example, around one in ten jobs in shipbuilding occupied by women.

This was not, however, entirely a triumph for gender equality. Although many women found their new work opportunities liberating, they were paid less than men for the same work and it was made clear that they could expect to lose their jobs when the men came back from the war. American women also served in ancillary roles in the armed forces, but there was a reluctance to send them overseas and few advanced beyond clerical duties.

Race in wartime America

On the US home front mobilization for total war presented new opportunities for black and Hispanic Americans. The insatiable demand for labour in factories in northern and western cities drew half a million black people away from the rural South. The black population of San Francisco grew from 5,000 to over 30,000, while in Detroit, a city already possessing a substantial African-American community, blacks increased by 60,000. Thousands of Mexican workers were also drawn into California. In June 1941 the Roosevelt administration's Fair Employment Practices order banned racial discrimination in defence industries and government jobs, but blacks continued to face gross prejudice. The American Red Cross refused blood donations from black people because white soldiers would not accept it. Racial tensions led to outbreaks of violence, notably the Detroit race riots of summer 1943 which left 34 dead. In the notorious Zoot Suit riots in Los Angeles in June 1943, white servicemen attacked young Mexicans sporting stylish clothing. Both black migration to cities and Mexican immigration were set to continue after the war's end.

Banners erected outside a federal housing project in Detroit, Michigan, in an attempt to prevent black tenants from moving in, 1942.

Segregation in the US forces

The United States fought a war to destroy the racist Nazi state with armed forces that were strictly racially segregated. Around one million African Americans served in the war. Placed under white officers, they were routinely consigned to support duties, for example serving as cooks, cleaners or construction workers. Every aspect of military life was segregated, from parades to canteens. Under pressure of military need, and also as a result of campaigning by civil rights groups, some black servicemen found a chance to perform in combat roles. The first African-American airmen, trained at Tuskegee in Alabama, performed with distinction as 332nd Fighter Group in Italy in 1944, escorting bombers in raids over Germany. In the army, black infantry under white officers were rushed into frontline combat during the crisis of the Battle of the Bulge in late 1944, and the 76th Tank Battalion, known as the Black Panthers, saw extensive action late in the war in Europe. But men who had fought as heroes for their country were still denied access to all-white rest and recreation facilities.

Tuskegee airmen adjust an external drop tank on the wing of an aircraft.

The internment of Japanese Americans

One of the most controversial US government actions of World War II was the internment of people of Japanese ethnicity, whether or not they were citizens of the United States. Under the Alien Enemies Act, the authorities were enabled to detain citizens of hostile countries. Many Germans and Italians were confined under this legislation, as well as Japanese. But only ethnic Japanese were deprived of their rights despite being US nationals. Executive Order 9066, signed by President Roosevelt in February 1942, permitted the relocation of ethnic Japanese from the Pacific coastal regions, where most of them lived, allegedly on security grounds, though no evidence existed of disloyal activity to justify the action. The clear racist basis for interning American-born ethnic Japanese was articulated in a *Los Angeles Times* editorial, which asserted that 'a viper is a viper wherever the egg is hatched'. Around 120,000 Japanese Americans were deported to camps in distant, mostly desolate areas of the United States, more than 60 per cent of them US citizens. They were released in 1945 but had lost their homes, farms and businesses.

Manzanar Relocation Center, California,
now a National Historic Site.

Japanese imperialism

In 1940 Japan faced an international situation full of worrying uncertainty, but also opportunities for imperial expansion. The country's gruelling war in China was placing great strain upon the economy. Supporting the Chinese Nationalists, the United States was already imposing trade restrictions on Japan. But the German victories in Europe in summer 1940 left the European colonies of Southeast Asia – French Indochina, the Dutch East Indies and British-ruled Malaya and Singapore – temptingly exposed to potential conquest. Japan's leaders had a vision of an Asian empire they dubbed 'the Greater East Asia Co-Prosperity Sphere', but its form and extent were vague. The Japanese Army leaned towards possible expansion in Mongolia and Siberia, but defeat by Soviet forces at Khalkhyn Gol in Mongolia in 1939 had shown a drive northwards was a tough option. The vulnerability of the colonial empires brought a southern strategy to the forefront. The seizure of Southeast Asia could make Japan self-sufficient in strategic materials such as oil and rubber, as well as improving the chances of victory in China. It was an almost irresistible prospect.

Japanese Emperor Hirohito rides his horse during an army inspection, 1938.

America confronts Japan

In September 1940 Japanese troops occupied the north of French Indochina, cutting supply routes to the Chinese army. In the same month, Japan signed a Tripartite Pact with Nazi Germany and Fascist Italy, making it a member of the Axis alliance. Both of these moves infuriated the United States. Roosevelt responded with ever tighter restrictions on Japanese trade and increased supplies to the Chinese Nationalists. The Japanese did not want war with America but nor did they wish to abandon their imperial ambitions. In April 1941 they signed a Neutrality Pact with the Soviet Union, in effect covering their backs for a southward strike.

In July 1941 Japanese troops entered Saigon, occupying all of French Indochina. Along with Britain and the Netherlands, the United States responded by imposing an economic blockade on Japan. Roosevelt demanded the Japanese withdraw troops not only from Indochina but also from China. Cut off from imported supplies of oil and other essentials, Japan faced a stark choice between war or surrender to American power.

Japanese troops enter Saigon in 1941.

Japan plans a war against the United States

When General Hideki Tojo became prime minister in October 1941, Japan still hoped to avoid war with the United States. The Japanese civilian and military leaders, who collectively took key decisions, were aware of the huge superiority of US resources. The young Emperor Hirohito discreetly expressed his desire for peace. But the search for a compromise with Washington came to nothing, primarily because the Americans wholly distrusted Japanese intentions. The effects of the economic blockade meant a decision could not be postponed endlessly. The Japanese leadership finally opted for war as a pessimistic gamble. They did not believe they would win, but they thought they had a chance. The plan that seemed to make Japanese victory at least feasible was devised by a naval officer, Admiral Isoroku Yamamoto. He advocated a devastating surprise strike against the US Pacific Fleet at Pearl Harbour, Hawaii. This would buy the Japanese time to occupy Southeast Asia and establish a defensive perimeter in the Pacific. The weakened US navy would be finished off and Americans persuaded to accept Japanese domination of Asia.

"I am looking forward to dictating peace to the United States in the White House at Washington"
— ADMIRAL YAMAMOTO

What do YOU say, AMERICA?

The attack on Pearl Harbor

At dawn on 7th December 1941 a first wave of 183 Japanese naval aircraft took off from six carriers north of Hawaii to attack the US fleet at Pearl Harbor. The carriers had crossed thousands of miles of ocean from Japan unobserved and their strike achieved complete surprise. Most of the US aircraft that should have defended the base were destroyed on the ground, allowing Japanese level bombers, dive-bombers and torpedo aircraft to wreak havoc on the moored warships. A second wave of 170 aircraft completed the mayhem. For trivial loss to the Japanese, 18 American warships were sunk or severely damaged, including five battleships, and 2,400 Americans killed.

The 'sneak' attack delivered without a declaration of war outraged American opinion. Any hope that America might in the future negotiate a compromise peace with Japan was lost from the start. The Pearl Harbor attack also fell short of its military objective, missing the Pacific Fleet's four aircraft carriers, which were at sea.

The surprise attack on Pearl Harbor. In his speech declaring war on 8th December, Roosevelt spoke of the event as 'a day of infamy'.

The tide of Japanese conquest

Synchronized with the attack on Pearl Harbor, the Japanese army launched offensives against British Malaya and the US-dominated Philippines. Controlling the ocean and the air, Japan carried out seaborne landings largely unopposed. Attempting to stop landings on the Malayan coast on 10th December, the British battleship *Prince of Wales* and battle cruiser *Repulse* were sunk by Japanese aircraft. This naval disaster left Malaya and the British base at Singapore exposed to fast-moving, highly motivated Japanese infantry. The Malayan campaign ended in Japanese victory after little over two months. In the Philippines, US and Filipino troops under General Douglas MacArthur were overwhelmed by Japanese invasion forces. Withdrawing to the Bataan peninsula, they held out until April 1942. Meanwhile, the Japanese proceeded with second-stage offensives to seize the Dutch East Indies and Burma. Another Japanese naval victory at the Java Sea at the end of February 1942 left them effectively unopposed in the Indian Ocean. As the British withdrew from Burma in May 1942, Japan controlled the empire it had sought.

USSR

Mongolia

Manchuria

Korea

China

Japan

| | Japanese-controlled territory, May 1942 |

Iwo Jima

Wake Islands

Okinawa

Mariana Islands

Burma

Formosa

Guam

Thailand

French Indo-China

Philippines

dia

Malaya

Palau Islands

Caroline Islands

Marshall Islands

Gilbert Islands

Dutch East Indies

New Guinea

Solomon Islands

Guadalcanal

The spread of Japan

The fall of Singapore

The naval base at Singapore, created in the 1930s, was the prime symbol of British imperial power in Southeast Asia. After the outbreak of war with Germany, however, it was starved of military equipment, Churchill giving priority not only to the defence of Britain, but also to the campaign in the North African desert. When the Japanese attacked Malaya in December 1941, the British had only a handful of obsolete aircraft to counter Japanese air power and, after the sinking of *Prince of Wales* and *Repulse*, few naval resources either. After a triumphant campaign on the Malay peninsula, Japanese troops crossed to Singapore island on the night of 8th–9th February 1942. The base was defended by 70,000 Australian, Indian and British troops under General Arthur Percival. The Japanese troops were only half that number, but they had superior equipment and morale, plus effective air support. Outfought, the defenders were soon forced back to a perimeter around the base. Utterly demoralized, Percival surrendered on 15th February. It was a humiliation from which British prestige in Asia never recovered.

The British surrender at Singapore, 1942.

The Bataan Death March

The Japanese made initial landings on Luzon, the largest island of the Philippines, on 10th December 1941, following up with a full-scale invasion 12 days later. The Philippines were defended by US and Filipino troops under General Douglas MacArthur. Unable to repel the landings, by 7th January 1942, MacArthur had withdrawn his forces to the craggy Bataan peninsula. There, they mounted a stubborn defence, aided by the Japanese transfer of their best troops to the invasion of the Dutch East Indies. On 12th March MacArthur was evacuated to Australia, announcing 'I will return', a promise he was eventually to keep. After heroic resistance, the cornered forces at Bataan surrendered on 9th April. Some 12,000 Americans and more than 60,000 Filipinos became prisoners of war. The Japanese decided to move this mass of men 145 km (90 miles) to Camp O'Donnell. Suffering brutal mistreatment, as many as 15,000 of them may have died travelling on foot and by train. Dubbed the 'Bataan Death March', this incident became, along with Pearl Harbor, the most famous reference point for American wartime hatred of the Japanese.

The Bataan Death March, 1942. Prisoners are forced to walk with their hands tied behind their backs.

The defence of Corregidor

The island of Corregidor in the mouth of Manila harbour was the site of the last US resistance to the Japanese takeover of the Philippines. Mainly constructed before World War I, the island's fortifications included a network of concrete tunnels and underground storerooms. A formidable array of guns, from long-range coastal artillery to anti-aircraft weaponry, provided its armoury. Under General Jonathan M Wainright, US commander in the Philippines after the withdrawal of General MacArthur, Corregidor continued to hold out after the fall of Bataan. Garrisoned by the US Marine's 4th Regiment and an assortment of other US and Filipino servicemen, it came under constant bombardment from the air and from Japanese army artillery. The defenders also suffered from severe shortages of food and water. On 5th May the Japanese launched seaborne landings on the island, but their troops still encountered fierce resistance. The following day, however, General Wainright reluctantly surrendered, stating: 'There is a limit of human endurance, and that point has long been passed'.

The Japanese land on the island of Corregidor, Philippines, 1942. The defence of Corregidor is credited with checking the previously unhindered momentum of the Japanese offensives.

Australia under attack

At the outbreak of World War II Australia placed its limited military resources unreservedly at the service of Britain. Australians were dispatched to fight in the Mediterranean, on the assumption the Royal Navy would guarantee the security of Australia itself. The loss of Malaya and Singapore, in which some 15,000 Australians were taken prisoner, left the country exposed. On 19th February 1942, four days after the fall of Singapore, several hundred Japanese carrier and land-based aircraft attacked the port of Darwin in Australia's Northern Territory, which was being used as an Allied base for operations in defence of the Dutch East Indies. Ships were sunk and port facilities destroyed.

Japan had no plans to invade Australia, but the shock to Australia was profound. Australian forces were withdrawn from the European war to serve under overall American command as part of the South West Pacific Area. A fundamental shift in Australian loyalties away from Britain and towards the United States had begun.

MV *Neptuna* explodes and clouds of smoke from oil storage tanks billow into the sky, during the Japanese air raid on Darwin.

The Doolittle Raid

After Pearl Harbor, President Roosevelt felt a direct strike against Japan itself was needed to lift morale. Aircraft carriers presented the only feasible means of launching such an attack, but they could not be risked close enough to Japan for a raid by naval aircraft. Instead a scheme was devised for long-range B-25 Mitchell bombers to take off from a carrier in the mid-Pacific, bomb Japan, and fly on to land at airfields in China controlled by pro-American forces. This mission was entrusted to famous veteran pilot Colonel James Doolittle. On 18th April 1942, aboard the carrier USS *Hornet*, 16 B-25s laden with bombs and fuel succeeded in getting airborne without loss, a remarkable feat. Flying 1,000 km (620 miles) to Japan, they bombed Tokyo and other cities in daylight, causing some 50 civilian deaths. None reached designated airfields in China. All the aircraft were lost but most aircrew survived crash-landing or bailing out. An unfortunate eight airmen who fell into Japanese hands were tortured by their captors. The raid had its intended effect, cheering the Americans and shocking the Japanese.

A B–25 Mitchell bomber takes off from the aircraft carrier USS *Hornet* during the Doolittle Raid.

The Battle of the Coral Sea

Advancing across the South Pacific, in April 1942 the Japanese sent troop convoys under naval escort into the Coral Sea, aiming to occupy Tulagi in the Solomons and Port Moresby in New Guinea. The US navy knew of Japanese intentions as it was reading their navy's radio traffic. A force including the carriers *Lexington* and *Yorktown* was sent to engage the Japanese, whose escort ships included the carriers *Shokaku* and *Zuikaku*. From 4th May a confused long-range battle was fought in often poor visibility. On 7th May American naval aircraft located and sank the light carrier *Shohu*. The following day, while their aircraft were away attacking *Shokaku*, *Yorktown* and *Lexington* were struck by Japanese dive-bombers and torpedo aircraft. *Yorktown* was severely damaged and *Lexington* had to be scuttled. It had been the first battle fought entirely by carrier aircraft, without the opposing ships sighting one another. The US navy fared the worst, but the Japanese were forced to abandon their planned landings at Port Moresby, a significant setback after their string of victories.

The US navy aircraft carrier USS *Lexington*, on fire during the latter part of the Japanese air attack on 8th May 1942.

The Battle of Midway

Admiral Isoroku Yamamoto intended to follow up the Pearl Harbor raid with a final battle in mid-Pacific to finish off the US fleet. He devised an elaborate plan to occupy Midway Island and lure the Americans into a disastrous naval counter-attack. The US navy learned of the scheme through decoded radio intercepts. Three carriers, *Hornet*, *Enterprise* and *Yorktown* – rapidly repaired after the Coral Sea – were sent to surprise the Japanese during their Midway operation. On 4th June the four Japanese carriers supporting the landings were attacked by waves of US carrier aircraft. The US torpedo planes were savaged by the Japanese carriers' Zero fighters, but the dive-bombers delivered attacks of devastating precision, reducing three of the carriers to burning wrecks. The surviving Japanese carrier *Hiryu* succeeded in flying off its aircraft to strike *Yorktown* before also being destroyed by dive-bombing later that day. The crippled *Yorktown* was subsequently sunk by a Japanese submarine, but Midway remained an overwhelming US victory. The Japanese Imperial Navy never fully recovered from the losses inflicted by the US naval aviators.

The scene onboard USS *Yorktown*, shortly after she was hit by three Japanese bombs on 4th June 1942.

Battle joined at Guadalcanal

In August 1942 America took the offensive in the Pacific War, seeking to build on the victory at Midway. Its target was the Solomon Islands, which the Japanese had already begun to occupy. On 7th August around 11,000 US Marines were landed on the island of Guadalcanal and others on neighbouring Tulagi. The Japanese Imperial Navy swiftly counter-attacked against the warships supporting the landings, sinking four Allied cruisers in a night battle off Savo Island. This naval disaster left the Marines ashore temporarily cut off and short of supplies.

Completing a half-built Japanese jungle airstrip, which they renamed Henderson Field, within two weeks the Marines were able to fly in planes to provide air cover. The Japanese landed troops on Guadalcanal, but in insufficient numbers to capture the island. Failing to establish naval superiority at the Battle of the Eastern Solomons in late August, the Japanese had to settle for a slow build-up, ferrying soldiers nightly to Guadalcanal on destroyers – an operation the Americans called the 'Tokyo Express'.

A patrol composed of fighting Leathernecks starts its trek on a mission at sunset on Guadalcanal, August 1942.

American victory at Guadalcanal

In late 1942 the fighting at Guadalcanal reached its climax. On 12th-13th September Japanese infantry launched near-suicidal attacks on a feature known as Edson's Ridge, but were repelled by the US Marines with heavy losses. This pushed the Japanese to redouble their efforts. The number of Japanese infantry on the island rose to over 20,000 by mid-October, while the Americans suffered from bombardment by sea and air, as well as from tropical heat and humidity. On 24th–26th October a major Japanese attack around Henderson Field was beaten off with heavy losses inflicted. Undeterred, in mid-November the Japanese planned further major troop landings. However, in a series of hard-fought night engagements known as the Naval Battle of Guadalcanal, two of their battleships were sunk. Eleven troop transports were also destroyed. Unable to match the American build-up of forces on the island, the Japanese reluctantly admitted failure and evacuated their troops from Guadalcanal in early 1943. US Admiral William Halsey wrote: 'Before Guadalcanal the enemy advanced at his pleasure – after Guadalcanal he retreated at ours.'

Debris from a Japanese landing boat and its sister ships
litters the shore on Guadalcanal Island.

Fighting in the New Guinea jungle

Although the Battle of the Coral Sea prevented landings at Port Moresby, New Guinea, the Japanese still sought to capture the town on the Papuan peninsula. In July 1942 they landed troops at Buna on the north coast and advanced south along the Kokoda Trail, an appallingly difficult track through mountains, swamps and jungle. The Japanese drove an opposing Australian force back to within 40 km (25 miles) of Port Moresby, while making further landings at Milne Bay at the tip of the peninsula. The Milne Bay landings were repulsed in early September and counter-attacking Australian and US troops drove the Japanese back northwards along the Kokoda Trail. On both sides hardship and disease caused heavier casualties than combat. By January 1943, after a last-ditch stand at Buna, the Japanese troops were overcome. Japan remained in control of Lae, to the west of Buna, but an attempt to reinforce the troops there in March 1943 resulted in disaster. A convoy of troop transports escorted by destroyers was attacked by Allied aircraft and torpedo boats in the Bismarck Sea and annihilated.

Australian infantry advance in an assault on Buna, 1943.

The continuing war in China

In 1942 two-fifths of the Japanese army was still engaged in the war in China, where Chiang Kai-shek's Nationalists and Mao Zedong's Communists, nominally allies, continued to resist from their remote bases in, respectively, Chongqing and Yan'an. After Pearl Harbor, Roosevelt approved massive military aid to the Nationalists and sent General Joseph Stilwell to oversee how it was used. Chiang Kai-shek was feted as a major ally, one of the 'Big Four' alongside Churchill, Stalin and Roosevelt. Disillusion soon set in. The Japanese occupation of Burma in April 1942 cut the supply route to the Nationalists – the famous 'Burma Road' – so all military equipment and fuel had to be flown in over the Himalayas. Stilwell found Nationalist generals keener on fighting the Communists and lining their own pockets than attacking the Japanese. At Yan'an the Communists were more active, organizing a peasant-based guerrilla campaign that provoked ferocious reprisals from Japanese troops with orders to 'kill all, burn all, loot all'. The stalemate in China was frustrating for the Allies but, for Japan, a disastrous drain on military resources.

Chiang Kai-shek (left) and General Stilwell at Maymyo, Burma, April 1942.

Biological warfare

Japan was the only country to use biological weapons in World War II. They were developed at the army's Unit 731 in Manchuria. Infectious agents, ranging from bubonic plague to anthrax, cholera and typhoid, were turned into sprays or ceramic bombs to be delivered by aircraft. The Japanese used these weapons exclusively against the Chinese. In 1940, for example, plague-infected fleas were dropped on Ningbo, provoking a major epidemic. In 1942 biological weapons were employed against peasants in Zhejiang, in retaliation for the aid local people gave to US airmen who had participated in the Doolittle Raid. Japanese biological warfare caused at least 400,000 deaths.

The world leaders in this field were, however, the British and Americans. Britain had biological weapons by 1941 and, building on British expertise, the US developed a major germ warfare facility in Maryland. After the Japanese surrender, several Unit 731 experts were given immunity from prosecution in return for supplying data from their experiments to the United States.

The derelict site of what once served as Japanese Unit 731, Harbin, China, where experiments were performed on human subjects under the direction of medical officer Shiro Ishii.

The Chindits

The Japanese conquest of Burma (Myanmar) in April 1942 took them to the limit of their intended advance in Asia. Burma's only strategic significance was as the potential route for supplies to Nationalist China. This was sufficient motive for the Allies to plot its recapture, but not sufficient to make them allocate resources adequate for the task. A weak British attack from India into Burma failed and plans for a major offensive coordinated with the Chinese came to nothing. In this frustrating situation a proposal by eccentric British brigadier Orde Wingate for Long-Range Penetration Groups, dubbed the Chindits, to operate behind enemy lines won official backing. Depending on airdropped supplies, the Chindits made an incursion into Burma in February–April 1943. They caused limited damage at the cost of 800 casualties, but the operation boosted morale. The following year the Chindits made a far more substantial incursion. Some 8,000 men, flown in by gliders and transport aircraft, engaged in fierce fighting with the Japanese. However, Wingate was killed and long-range penetration was sidelined as larger-scale conventional fighting took over.

THE CHINDIT BADGE
PORTRAYING A CHINTHE, A MYTHICAL
BEAST, GUARDIAN OF BURMESE TEMPLES

The badge of the Chindits on the Chindit memorial outside
the Ministry of Defence building in London, England.

The Burma Railway

Invaded by Japanese troops in December 1941, Thailand signed a treaty with Japan and declared war on the Allies. In June 1942 the Japanese decided to build a railway to carry supplies across Thailand to their forces in Burma. The line would stretch 420 km (260 miles) through jungle terrain and required construction of some 600 bridges. Work began in September 1942. Around 250,000 Asians, chiefly Burmese and Malayans, provided the main body of the labour force. Alongside them worked 61,000 Allied prisoners of war, including Australians, British and Dutch, captured in the fall of Singapore and other early Japanese victories. The line was finished in October 1943, a rapid completion achieved through imposing a brutal rhythm of work upon the labourers. Short of food and without medicines, subjected to routine abuse and casual cruelty by their guards, driven to work when sick, about 16,000 POWs died building the railway. The death rate among Asian labourers was even higher, an estimated 90,000 losing their lives. After the defeat of Japan, the building of the line was designated a war crime.

Bridge over the Kwai River, Kanchanaburi, Thailand.

India in turmoil

There was a brief panic in British India when Japanese carrier aircraft attacked Ceylon (Sri Lanka) in April 1942, but the real threat to British rule in the subcontinent came from the local population. At the start of World War II, leaders of the Indian nationalist movement expressed lukewarm support for Britain. About two million Indians volunteered to serve in the British Indian army. But British defeats in Europe and Asia brought a change of mood. A radical nationalist, Subhas Chandra Bose sought the support of Nazi Germany and Japan. Bose became the leader of the Indian National Army (INA), a force consisting chiefly of Indian prisoners of war captured by the Japanese. The INA fought the British in Burma in 1944, but never numbered more than 45,000 men. Meanwhile, in August 1942 Mahatma Gandhi and his colleagues launched the Quit India campaign calling for immediate independence. The nationalist leadership was swiftly arrested, but widespread protests, strikes and acts of sabotage lasted into 1944. By the war's end, Britain had realized its rule in the Indian subcontinent could not endure.

Indians blockade rail traffic during the civil disobedience campaign encouraged by Mahatma Gandhi, 1945.

The Bengal famine

In 1943 a famine in Bengal killed an estimated three million of Britain's Indian subjects. Like all famines it had multiple causes. A poor harvest was partially to blame. The Japanese occupation of Burma denied Bengal access to a traditional source of rice imports and Japanese attacks on merchant shipping disrupted trade. But British wartime policies contributed largely to the disaster. In parts of Bengal thought at risk of Japanese invasion from Burma, the British impounded rice stocks and destroyed boats to deny them to the potential invaders. India's internal trade was disrupted by the war effort. Food supplies to the army and war workers were prioritized over food for peasants. Inflation driven by military spending made food unaffordable for the rural poor. Focused on the war and on combatting civil unrest, the British authorities were woefully slow to respond to the crisis. Churchill had an irrational dislike of Indians and blocked plans to allocate shipping to Bengal. A substantial relief effort got underway in October 1943, followed by a good harvest, but too late to prevent mass death.

A mother in shreds of clothing begs on the streets of Calcutta, 1943.

The SOE promotes resistance

Soon after the fall of France in June 1940, Churchill ordered the creation of a secret organization to promote resistance in German-occupied Europe. Called the Special Operations Executive (SOE), it was formed under the aegis of the Ministry of Economic Warfare and instructed to 'go and set Europe ablaze'. As the SOE was initially built up through the 'old boy network' of the privately-educated elite, a spirit of enthusiastic amateurism pervaded the organization. Agents were recruited chiefly among foreign exiles in Britain. The SOE established contact with nascent resistance groups and sent agents to train them as radio operators and saboteurs – parachuted in or landed at night on improvised airstrips aboard Lysander aircraft. Poor security allowed German intelligence to penetrate the operation in the Netherlands, with disastrous results, but as resistance movements grew the SOE in general provided important moral and material support. By 1944 the organization had a staff of more than 10,000 and was running operations across Europe from Norway to Greece.

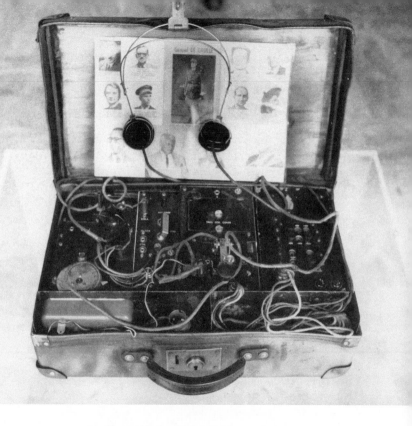

A radio used by Pierre Le Chene, a British secret
agent of the Special Operations Executive.

The assassination of Reinhard Heydrich

One of the most important men in Nazi Germany, Reinhard Heydrich was the deputy head of the SS and, from September 1941, 'Protector' of Bohemia and Moravia – what was left of the former Czechoslovakia. The SOE and the Czech government-in-exile in London devised a plan to assassinate Heydrich, an action they believed would stimulate resistance to Nazi occupation among the Czech population. Having trained with the SOE, nine members of the Czech army-in-exile were parachuted into Czech territory at the end of December. On 27th May 1942, Josef Gabcik and Jan Kubis ambushed Heydrich's car in a Prague street. Wounded by a grenade, he died eight days later. The Czech agents were betrayed and all died after a firefight with the SS in a church. Nazi reprisals against the Czech population included the destruction of the villages of Lidice and Lezaky. At Lidice the entire male population, numbering almost 200, was executed and the women and children were deported to camps where most died. It is estimated that a total of 5,000 Czechs were killed in Nazi reprisals.

Terence Cuneo's rendition of the assassination of Reinhard Heydrich.

The St Nazaire raid

In summer 1940 the British established Combined Operations Headquarters to organize raids on the coast of occupied Europe, while the Commandos were formed as a specialized raiding force. Little was achieved until the raid on the German-held French port of St Nazaire in March 1942. St Nazaire was the only Atlantic port with a dry dock large enough to repair capital ships such as the battleship *Tirpitz*. On 27th March the ageing destroyer *Campbeltown*, her bows packed with explosives, sailed for France accompanied by smaller vessels carrying Commandos. In the early hours of 28th March the convoy entered the estuary leading to the port, flying a German flag as deception. They eventually came under heavy fire but *Campbeltown* succeeded in ramming the dock gates and Commandos went ashore, engaging German troops and sabotaging dock facilities. Later in the day, after the fighting had stopped, a timer detonated *Campbeltown*'s explosives, destroying the dock gates and killing over 300 German soldiers and French civilians. The dock was permanently disabled, at the cost of some 400 British killed or captured.

Campbeltown during and after the raid.

The raid on Dieppe

In August 1942, British Combined Operations Headquarters decided to mount a large-scale raid on the French Channel port of Dieppe. The purpose of the raid was apparently to gain experience in amphibious operations in preparation for a future invasion of Europe. The main body of troops assigned to the raid were Canadians who had been sent to Britain but had not yet seen action.

Launched on 19th August, the raid was a fiasco. Naval gunfire failed to seriously damage German shore defences, and troops on the landing beaches found themselves trapped under heavy fire. Supporting tanks became bogged down in shingle. Only small-scale attacks by Commandos on the flanks of the landings achieved any success. Out of 5,000 Canadian engaged, 900 were killed, 600 wounded and 1,900 taken prisoner, an overall loss rate of 70 per cent. There were also substantial losses of aircraft and naval shipping. It was a painful way of learning that the Allies were as yet utterly incapable of invading occupied Europe.

In the wake of the raid, Churchill tanks and the bodies
of Allied servicemen scatter the beach at Dieppe.

The British bombing offensive

At the start of the war, the RAF's Bomber Command was restricted to attacks on naval targets to avoid killing civilians. As the war escalated, from May 1940, the bombers were ordered to strike industrial targets such as synthetic oil plants and railway yards in the Ruhr, but they could not achieve sufficient accuracy. Forced to fly by night to avoid slaughter by Luftwaffe fighters, they rarely struck within 8 km (5 miles) of their targets. The experience of the Blitz ended British inhibitions about causing German civilian casualties. In February 1942 Bomber Command came under a new leader, Air Chief Marshall Sir Arthur Harris. With a brief from the government to undermine 'the morale of the enemy civil population', Harris focused on 'area bombing' – indiscriminate attacks on cities. Equipped with new Lancaster and Halifax four-engine aircraft, as well as new navigational aids, Bomber Command began to hit its much-enlarged targets. In May and June 1942 highly publicized Thousand-Bomber Raids on Cologne and Essen showed the campaign to devastate German cities had begun in earnest.

Air Chief Marshall Arthur Harris, pictured in his office in London, May 1942.

The Dambusters

The dams that provided electricity and water to the Ruhr, Germany's industrial heartland, were a tempting target for strategic bombing. The installations were protected by anti-aircraft artillery and torpedo nets. An inventive British engineer, Barnes Wallis, devised a scheme for attacking the dams using a 'bouncing bomb'. Dropped from low altitude the 4,000 kg (9,000 lb) bomb would skip over the torpedo nets and explode underwater against the dam wall. The RAF adopted the scheme and created 617 Squadron to carry it out. After intensive training in precision low-level attack, 19 Lancaster bombers under Wing Commander Guy Gibson headed for the dams on the night of 16th–17th May 1943. After a series of bomb runs under heavy fire, the Möhne and Eder dams were breached, but the attack on the Sorpe dam failed. Some 1,500 people were killed in the flooding of the Ruhr valley and temporary disruption caused to industrial production. The RAF lost eight Lancasters. The 'Dambusters' raid was above all a boost to British morale. Gibson was awarded the Victoria Cross and feted as a war hero.

Lancaster bomber

The bombing of Hamburg

RAF Bomber Command leader Sir Arthur Harris firmly believed destroying Germany's cities was the way to victory – a series of devastating hammer-blows would force the Nazis to surrender. The strength of German air defences generally prevented this theory being tested. In July 1943, however, British night bombers attacking the port city of Hamburg used a new trick, scattering aluminium-foil strips to block German radar. Effectively blinded by this unexpected tactic, German night fighters and anti-aircraft guns were rendered ineffectual. On the night of 27th–28th July, 735 bombers dropped a mix of explosive and incendiary devices on the centre of the city. Aided by local weather conditions, the bombing stoked a firestorm that devastated a wide urban area, killing an estimated 40,000 people, mostly civilians. In the aftermath Albert Speer, Hitler's Minister of War Production, told the Führer that 'six more Hamburgs' would bring Germany to its knees. But RAF Bomber Command did not have the power to deliver such repeated blows. It would only achieve such absolute devastation of a city once more, at Dresden in February 1945.

An aerial view of
Hamburg taken on
the night of the raid.

US daylight bombing tactics

In 1942 elements of the US Eighth Air Force began arriving at bases in eastern England. The Americans were committed to strategic bombing as a form of economic warfare, aiming at precise industrial targets. This meant attacking by daylight. Their chief bomber aircraft, the B-17 Flying Fortress and the B-24 Liberator, were heavily armed – a B-17G mounted 13 machine guns. No existing Allied fighter had the range to escort raids deep into Germany. The bombers were to fly in mass formations at high altitude, holding off enemy fighters with their interlocking firepower. They would 'shoot their way in and shoot their way out'. At 2,750 kg (6,000 lb) and 4,400 kg (8,800 lb), their bombloads were inferior to those of an RAF Lancaster (6,350 kg/14,000 lb). Nonetheless, in a mass attack they delivered a formidable punch. Their sophisticated Norden bombsights would theoretically ensure they hit their precision targets, but this did not allow for operating under ground fire in cloud and mist. In effect the USAAF would bomb civilians because sufficient accuracy was never achieved.

B-17G Flying Fortress

The Schweinfurt and Regensburg raids

In June 1943 the 'Pointblank' directive ordered RAF and USAAF bombers to focus on crippling Germany's aircraft industry. Consequently, the USAAF planned a mass raid on two targets in Bavaria, southern Germany: the aircraft factory at Regensburg and the ball-bearing factory at Schweinfurt - ball-bearings being essential aircraft components. On 17th August 1943 two waves of B-17s, totalling 376 aircraft, took off from England for the long flight to Bavaria. The attacks on the two sites were supposed to be coordinated but instead went in hours apart. The B-17s attacking Regensburg mostly found their target, despite losses to fighter attack and flak. The survivors flew on to land in North Africa. The raid on Schweinfurt was an unmitigated failure, most bombs landing nowhere near the factory. Flying a round trip from England, the B-17s were savaged by German fighters. In total 60 B-17s were shot down and 11 so badly damaged they were written off. Almost 500 aircrew were lost. It was a stark demonstration of the difficulty of translating the theory of precision daylight bombing into practice.

The Boeing B–17F
formation over
Schweinfurt, Germany,
17th August 1943.

Bombing the Romanian oilfields

The refineries at the Ploesti oilfields in Romania provided about one-third of all Germany's wartime needs for petrol and other petroleum derivatives. Without this supply the German war machine would be crippled. Attacking Ploesti was, however, a daunting prospect for the US bombers. In 1943 the oilfields could only be reached by the B-24 Liberators of USAAF Ninth Air Force based in North Africa. A plan was devised for B-24s to fly the 4,345-km (2,700-mile) trip to Ploesti and back, bombing the refineries at very low altitude, and using delayed-action bombs so the aircraft would not be wrecked by their own explosives.

On 1st August 1943, 178 Liberators were assembled for the operation. A complex plan for various groups of bombers to attack different refineries degenerated into chaos as the low-level attack went in under intense fire from 88 mm anti-aircraft guns and machine guns. Estimates of American losses vary, but as many as 73 B-24s probably failed to return and 310 aircrew were killed. Most of the damage to the refineries was swiftly repaired.

B-24 Liberators approach the oil refineries at Ploesti, Romania.

Winning the air war over Germany

From late 1943 through 1944, the Allies won the struggle for air superiority over Germany, although it was a hard-fought victory. The RAF battled on at night, still suffering appalling losses in mass raids on Berlin and Nuremberg through the winter of 1943–44. For the Americans, a turning point was the provision of long-range fighter escorts, chiefly P-51 Mustang fighters, for daylight bombing raids. By the start of the 'Big Week' American raids in February 1944, the USAAF could field a thousand bombers at a time under effective escort. After a break during which most bomber resources were devoted to the preparations for D-Day, the bombing of Germany resumed in earnest from late summer 1944. The scale, frequency and effectiveness of raids was now far greater as German air defences were eroded. The Ploesti oilfields finally stopped production in August after 24 raids. By the end of the year most German cities were in ruins. The Combined Bomber Offensive was at last achieving its main stated objective, 'the destruction and dislocation of the German military, industrial and economic systems'.

'The enemy can see your light: dim them!'

German war production

In 1942 Hitler appointed architect Albert Speer as Minister of Armaments and War Production, and German output of war materiel rose steeply. Between 1942 and 1944 production of aircraft almost tripled and the number of tanks built quadrupled, despite the Allied bombing campaign. As in Allied countries, labour and resources were diverted from civilian to military production and women were recruited for factory work on a large scale – by 1944 one-third of German munitions workers were women. But Germany also benefitted from the ruthless exploitation of forced labour – inmates of the concentration camps, workers conscripted from conquered countries, and prisoners of war.

To cope with Allied bombing, industries were dispersed in scattered smaller factories that made more difficult targets. Some production was shifted into caves or vast purpose-built underground facilities. It was not until late 1944 that the scale and effectiveness of Allied bombing sent the German war economy into terminal decline.

Albert Speer

German air defences

Germany deployed large-scale resources in the defence of its cities. One-quarter of artillery was devoted to anti-aircraft duties, as were the Luftwaffe's best pilots and fighter aircraft. Diverting these resources away from the army frontline was probably Allied strategic bombing's most crucial contribution to winning the war. Night fighting over Germany became a contest in technical ingenuity. German fighters were initially guided to attack RAF bombers by radar-equipped ground controllers, but then aircraft such as the Messerschmitt 110 were given airborne radar. The RAF developed radar-jamming techniques as counter-measures. Some fighters were mounted with vertical upward-firing cannon, to fire into the bellies of bombers flying above them. Attacking the American daylight bombers required less ingenuity but equal skill and courage. Luftwaffe pilots generally emerged victorious from encounters with massed B-17s until the Americans introduced fighter escorts in 1944. The Luftwaffe suffered a rapid and fatal erosion of its strength thereafter, through the loss of experienced pilots and fuel shortages.

German anti-aircraft gun

The first jet aircraft

The Luftwaffe staged the first flight by a prototype jet aircraft, the Heinkel He-178, five days before the outbreak of World War II. Development of a useable military jet was painfully slow. Hitler demanded production of a jet bomber, which he saw as a wonder weapon that might win the war, but only a fighter was feasible. The Messerschmitt Me 262 Schwalbe jet fighter finally entered service in spring 1944, deployed in defence of German cities. About 160 kmh (100 mph) faster than any propeller-driven aircraft, the Me 262 proved a highly effective interceptor, shooting down more than 500 Allied aircraft by the war's end. However, reliability problems, fuel shortages and Allied air superiority prevented it having any decisive impact. Germany also deployed the even faster Me 163 Komet rocket aircraft from May 1944, but to very limited effect.

The RAF had its own jet fighter, the Gloster Meteor, operational from July 1944, employed to intercept V-1 flying bombs over southern England.

Messerschmitt Me 262

The bombing of Dresden

By February 1945 the Allied air forces had achieved command of the skies over Germany. The largely untouched city of Dresden was chosen as a target because it was a railway and road centre through which German troops and materiel could move to the Eastern Front. On the night of 13th–14th February RAF Bomber Command sent more than 700 heavy bombers to attack the city with explosives and incendiaries, triggering a devastating firestorm. Follow-up attacks by the USAAF and RAF completed the destruction. An estimated 25,000 people were killed.

The attack on Dresden became a focus for critics of the morality of area bombing and Churchill distanced himself from a policy he had wholeheartedly advocated. It should not obscure the fact that the bomber offensive was one of the hardest-fought campaigns of the war. RAF Bomber Command lost 56,000 men, almost half of all aircrew who took part. The USAAF Eighth Air Force bombing campaign cost 26,000 American lives. Recent estimates suggest 350,000 German civilians were killed by Allied bombing.

Overlooking the destroyed city from the Rathaus (town hall).

Stalingrad: holding the city

On the Eastern Front, General Friedrich Paulus's Sixth Army, advancing on the left flank of the German thrust into the Caucasus, reached the outskirts of Stalingrad on the Volga River in mid-August 1942. After a Luftwaffe mass-bombing raid reduced most of the city to ruins, German troops expected to occupy it in a few days. But Stalin ordered the city that bore his name to be held at all costs. Under General Vasili Chuikov, Soviet forces mounted a ferociously determined defence, building by building and street by street. With the opposing forces only a few metres apart, superior German firepower could not be brought to bear – snipers were more effective than tanks or artillery. Resupplied from the far bank of the Volga, where Chuikov had his command post, Soviet troops clung on. A grain silo was held by its Soviet defenders, under siege for two months. By mid-November the Soviets occupied only isolated enclaves backing on to the river, yet this was enough to deny Paulus the victory he needed and to provide the time for a crushing counter-offensive.

The dancing figures of the Barmaley Fountain
stand in the wake of the battle, 1943.

Stalingrad: Germany defeated

Soviet General Georgy Zhukov devised a bold plan to trap Paulus's German Sixth Army in Stalingrad. He assembled a million men north and south of the city and, on 19th November 1942, launched them against Romanian and Hungarian troops holding the flanks of the Axis salient. Zhukov's pincers closed behind Sixth Army, which was cut off from reinforcement and resupply. Hitler refused to allow Paulus to fight his way out of the city, insisting he hold on until relieved, but in December a German counter-offensive from outside failed to break the Soviet ring of steel. Under worsening winter conditions, the Luftwaffe could only fly in a small fraction of the food, munitions and fuel the encircled troops required. German soldiers began to starve and freeze to death. At the end of January 1943 Hitler promoted Paulus to field marshal, encouraging him to choose death rather than imprisonment, but on 2nd February the commander surrendered with his army. Paulus was one of the few Germans taken prisoner at Stalingrad who survived captivity. Total Axis losses in and around Stalingrad totalled some 800,000 men.

German prisoners of war captured during the Battle of Stalingrad.

General Zhukov

Soviet General Georgy Zhukov had to cope not only with fighting the enemy, but also with handling Stalin, whose suspicious and vindictive nature made life perilous even for a successful commander. Zhukov first showed his mastery of aggressive combined arms warfare defeating the Japanese at Khalkhyn Gol in Mongolia in 1939. Soviet chief of staff at the time of the Axis invasion in 1941, he was sacked for openly disagreeing with Stalin's strategy. Recalled to lead the defence of Leningrad and then of Moscow, he regained the dictator's confidence and was appointed deputy supreme commander – the supreme commander was Stalin himself. The success of Zhukov's encirclement of the Germans at Stalingrad confirmed his status as a Soviet hero. His handling of the crucial battle of Kursk in July 1943, turning stubborn defence into a crushing counter-attack, was a master class in field command. Leading the sustained offensives that eventually took Soviet troops to Berlin, Zhukov ended the war with greater personal prestige than Stalin could tolerate. He was demoted to obscure peacetime postings until after the dictator's death.

The Battle of Kursk

After the German defeat at Stalingrad the war in the Soviet Union remained finely balanced. Hitler authorized a summer offensive in 1943 to regain the initiative. Forces under General Erich von Manstein were to carry out a pincer movement to encircle Soviet troops in a salient around the city of Kursk. Anticipating the attack, Soviet General Zhukov fortified the salient with minefields, trenches, anti-tank guns and artillery. He also assembled a large armoured reserve ready for a counter-offensive. The Germans attacked on 4th July, but their offensive stalled in the face of the well-prepared Soviet defences. When Zhukov unleashed his massed armour from 12th July, a titanic tank battle was fought, in which the more numerous Soviet T-34s eventually overcame the superior German Tigers and Panthers. Involving some three million men and 10,000 tanks, the Battle of Kursk ended in late August with the Germans in full retreat. The Soviet Union had suffered massive losses but it could replace its casualties and lost equipment, while Germany could not. The Red Army advanced unstoppably westward, reaching Kiev in November.

T-34 tanks on their way out of the factory and heading for battle.

The British victory at El Alamein

In October 1942 the British Eighth Army changed the course of the Desert War. Blocked in their advance into Egypt, Rommel's Panzerarmee Afrika had settled into a strong defensive position at El Alamein. Eighth Army commander General Bernard Montgomery patiently built up his forces until he had 200,000 men and 1,000 tanks, double the strength of Rommel's forces. Informed by Enigma intelligence, the British knew the Axis forces were experiencing serious supply problems. Rommel was absent on sick leave when, on 23rd October, Montgomery attacked. He planned to lock the Axis forces into a grinding attritional struggle. Eighth Army infantry advanced through minefields under cover of a 600-gun artillery barrage. Progress was slow, British armour sustaining heavy losses to German anti-tank guns. Rommel returned and launched a counter-offensive that failed. After a week's fighting New Zealand infantry penetrated the north of the Axis line. As Montgomery's reserve armour broke through, by 4th November the Axis forces were falling back in disorder. Montgomery pursued in methodical fashion, content to drive Rommel westward.

A member of a German tank crew surrenders as British infantry rush his tank at El Alamein, 27th October 1942.

General Montgomery

General Bernard Montgomery became commander of British Eighth Army by accident. Seeking a more aggressive leader for the desert forces in August 1942, Churchill appointed General William Gott to the post, but Gott's aircraft was shot down and he was killed. Chosen as replacement, Montgomery resisted Churchill's urgings to launch a premature attack, working to improve Eighth Army's morale and training. Having learned his trade on the Western Front in World War I, he preferred the systematic application of superior force to bold manoeuvre, but he combined this caution with a flamboyant showmanship that won the confidence of his troops. Although the victory at El Alamein made him a British hero, some American commanders heartily disliked both his personality and his generalship. He could be prickly to deal with and his methodical approach to battle could appear slow-moving and unimaginative. He did, however, get results. Montgomery's only disaster as a general was the wholly untypical Operation Market Garden in 1944, a bold airborne assault in which caution was thrown to the wind.

The Torch landings

The United States was reluctant to involve itself in the war in North Africa, which it regarded as an unnecessary sideshow in the fight against Hitler. However, persuaded by the British that an attempt to invade Europe would be premature, in autumn 1942 the Americans agreed to invade French North Africa. It was hoped that the Vichy authorities in Algeria and Morocco would not resist.

Some troops were brought direct from the United States, while an Anglo-American force sailed from Britain. Commanded by General Dwight D Eisenhower, the troops landed on 8th November at sites around Casablanca, Algiers and Oran. The landings were code-named Operation Torch. In the event, local forces put up some stiff resistance before, on 10th November, Vichy Admiral François Darlan ordered them to join the Allies. A complex political crisis followed, in which Darlan was assassinated by an anti-Vichy Frenchman and America attempted to place its own choice for Free French leader, General Henri Giraud, in control of French forces.

Invading North Africa

Axis surrender in Tunisia

In response to the Torch landings, in November 1942 Axis forces occupied Tunisia. There the Americans had their first experience of fighting the Germans. At the Kasserine Pass in February 1943 a counter-attack by Rommel's tanks drove the Americans into a panic retreat before the situation was stabilized. But the strategic position of the Axis forces in North Africa was increasingly hopeless, trapped between Montgomery's Eighth Army advancing from the east and Eisenhower's troops to the west. Hitler's irrational decision to send reinforcements into Tunisia only placed more men in jeopardy.

In March Montgomery attacked and overcame the fortified Mareth Line in southern Tunisia. Action by Allied naval and air forces cut Axis supply lines across the Mediterranean. The cities of Tunis and Bizerta fell to British and US troops on 7th May and Axis resistance ceased five days later. About 240,000 German and Italian soldiers surrendered, as many as were captured at Stalingrad. Rommel escaped, called home before the final debacle.

A Grant tank advances to support US forces during the battle at
Kasserine Pass, Tunisia, 1943.

The U-boat menace overcome

By summer 1942 the commander of the German submarine fleet Admiral Karl Dönitz had 140 U-boats available to attack the transatlantic convoys essential to Britain's survival and to US participation in the European war. Winston Churchill later wrote that the U-boat peril was 'the only thing that ever really frightened me during the war'. The Allies lost more than six million tonnes of shipping to submarine attacks in 1942 and sinkings continued to rise, reaching a critical level in March 1943, when 82 Allied ships were sunk in the Atlantic.

A sudden dramatic rise in the destruction of U-boats turned the Battle of the Atlantic around. A combination of factors for this included improved radar and radio direction-finding equipment for convoy escort ships, more extensive patrols by anti-submarine aircraft, and progress in Ultra code-breaking. Fifteen U-boats were sunk in the Atlantic in April and 34 in May, with relatively little damage inflicted on Allied ships. Dönitz admitted defeat, withdrawing his surviving submarines from the North Atlantic.

A depth charge explodes in the Atlantic Ocean, 1943.

The Casablanca Conference

In January 1943 Churchill, Roosevelt and their chiefs of staff flew to Casablanca, Morocco, for a summit meeting with significant consequences. The Americans arrived determined to press for an invasion of northern Europe, also demanded by the Soviet Union as a 'second front'. The British, who feared a premature cross-Channel invasion would fail, cannily persuaded their Allies to commit to landings in Sicily, knowing that this would not leave adequate resources for the northern operation as well. The Allies also agreed to mount a Combined Bomber Offensive against Germany, but the most significant decision was unilaterally imposed by Roosevelt. The president insisted on a public commitment to pursue 'unconditional surrender'. Germany and Japan were to be utterly defeated militarily, with no compromise or peace negotiations. This rigid stance was mostly intended to solidify the alliance with the Soviet Union, allaying Stalin's suspicions that the Western Allies might make a separate peace with Germany. But it may have lengthened the war, forcing the Germans and Japanese into a fight-to-the-death mentality.

Henri Giraud, Franklin D Roosevelt, Charles de Gaulle and Winston Churchill in Casablanca.

The invasion of Sicily

The Allied invasion of Sicily began on the night of 9th–10th July 1943, with assaults by airborne forces that were severely disrupted by gale-force winds. The weather also caused problems for the seaborne landings, but demoralized Italian troops provided only limited opposition. Once ashore, US General George Patton's army advanced along the west of the island and Montgomery's along the east. Axis forces, strengthened by elite German formations, put up stiff resistance in mountainous terrain.

Patton made faster progress than Montgomery, taking Palermo on 22nd July and then pressing towards Messina, officially a British target. Patton reached Messina a few hours before the British, but both Allied forces were too late to stop German commander General Albert Kesselring evacuating 100,000 Axis troops across the straits to the Italian mainland. Fighting on the island ceased on 17th August. Meanwhile, Italian King Victor Emmanuel had Mussolini arrested and a new government under Marshal Pietro Badoglio began seeking an armistice.

Troops unload supplies on the opening day of the Allied invasion of Sicily, 10th July 1943. The invasion involved 3,000 ships and 150,000 Allied troops.

Italy invaded

On 8th September 1943, General Eisenhower announced that an armistice had been concluded with Italy. The following day US and British troops under the command of General Mark Clark landed on beaches at Salerno on Italy's west coast. Any hopes that the Italian surrender would render the operation a walkover were swiftly dispelled. German land and air forces fiercely resisted the invasion, which came close to being driven back to the sea by a determined counter-offensive.

After Clark's army joined up with Montgomery's Eighth Army, which had made its own landings at Reggio and Taranto, the Allied forces began advancing up the Italian peninsula. Naples was occupied on 1st October, but German commander Kesselring prepared a strong defensive position, the Gustav Line, to block the Allies' path to Rome. Difficult terrain, worsening weather and stubborn German resistance had brought the Allies to a halt by December. Advocating the invasion of Italy, Churchill had called it the 'soft underbelly of Europe'. It had proved to be nothing of the kind.

American troops travel through Naples in
British trucks on their way to the front, 1943.

The Germans rescue Mussolini

Discredited by military defeats culminating in the Allied invasion of Sicily, on 25th July 1943 dictator Benito Mussolini was dismissed from power and arrested. When the new Italian government's armistice with the Allies was announced on 8th September, German forces acted swiftly to take over most of Italy and Italian-held territory abroad. The king and his government fled Rome, taking refuge with the Allies in southern Italy. On 12th September a small force of German Waffen-SS soldiers and paratroopers led by Captain Otto Skorzeny landed in gliders at the hotel in the Gran Sasso mountains where Mussolini was being held prisoner. They carried Mussolini off to northern Italy where he established a German-backed Fascist republic based at the town of Salo on Lake Garda. The north and centre of Italy descended into civil war as a major resistance movement, swelling in number to around half a million partisans, fought against Mussolini's Fascist army and the German occupiers. Meanwhile, the relatively small forces remaining under the command of the Italian royal government served alongside the Allies as 'co-belligerents'.

German paratroopers release Mussolini from his imprisonment at the Hotel Campo Imperatore, Gran Sasso, Italy, 1943.

The battle for Monte Cassino

The dominating heights of Monte Cassino, capped by a medieval Benedictine monastery, were the kingpin of the German Gustav defensive line that, at the start of 1944, blocked Allied progress towards Rome. Dug into bunkers and strongpoints, German elite troops ensured the position would be almost impossible to take by assault. On 11th January US and Free French troops attacked Monte Cassino but after prolonged fighting the operation failed. On 15th February it was the turn of New Zealand and Indian infantry of British Eighth Army to make the attempt. In preparation, at the request of the British, US bombers flattened the historic monastery. Much criticized at the time, the air bombardment merely created ruins that served as excellent cover for German troops. The February assault on Monte Cassino proved a costly failure as did another launched in mid-March. The Polish Corps, serving with Eighth Army, had the distinction of finally occupying the hilltop after a week's fierce fighting on 18th May. By that time the Germans had already decided on the need for a full-scale withdrawal northward.

Soldiers of the 2nd Polish Corps in the battle for Monte Cassino.

The landings at Anzio

In an attempt to break the deadlock on the Italian front, on 22nd January 1944 the Allies carried out amphibious landings at Anzio, between the German Gustav Line and Rome. Commanded by US General John Lucas, the US and British troops came ashore unopposed, achieving complete surprise. Aware of German dispositions through Enigma intelligence, senior commanders urged Lucas to press forward into the undefended territory in front of him. Instead, the cautious general consolidated a defensive perimeter around his beachhead. Reacting with their habitual speed, the Germans soon had the landing force trapped with its back to the sea. Churchill commented: 'I had hoped that we were hurling a wildcat onto the shore, but all we got was a stranded whale.' Lucas was replaced by General Lucien Truscott but the Allied troops remained pinned down under heavy fire from German artillery, mounting costly breakout attempts to no avail. Instead of the Anzio landings forcing a German withdrawal from the Gustav Line, it was the German retreat in late May that relieved the Allies from their hopeless position at Anzio.

Italian Front, January 1944

The fall of Rome

In mid-May 1944 German commander General Kesselring decided that the Gustav Line, penetrated by Free French colonial troops at its western end, could no longer be held. He ordered his troops to withdraw towards Rome. There was a real possibility that Allied forces could manoeuvre to encircle the retreating German forces, producing a major victory, but US General Mark Clark, commanding Fifth Army, had his eyes fixed on the prestige of a triumphal entry into the Italian capital. This he achieved on 5th June, although ironically the news of the event was entirely upstaged by the Normandy landings the following day.

In early August the Allies took Florence and towards the end of the month they penetrated another set of well-prepared German defences, the Gothic Line. Still their advance in central Italy stopped short of Bologna in October, and promising progress up the east coast halted after the fall of Ravenna in early December. Costing the Allies heavy casualties for limited results, the Italian campaign had become a sideshow.

The liberation of Rome, 1944. Armoured Allies march to Piazza Venezia, with its monument to King Vittorio Emanuele II of Savoy.

French resistance grows

Although involving a minority of the French population, during 1943 resistance grew into a movement with hundreds of thousands of adherents, all risking torture and death if captured. The introduction of compulsory labour service in February 1943, forcing young French people to engage in war work in Germany or on German projects in France, drove many to flee into hiding in remote country districts. Supplied with equipment by the British, these fugitives formed armed guerrilla groups, known as the 'maquisards', numbering over 40,000 by 1944. The Nazis delegated much of the work of suppressing the Resistance to the French paramilitary Milice, formed by the Vichy government in January 1943. In southern France fighting between the Milice and the 'maquis' guerrillas developed into a vicious civil war. The numerically much larger urban Resistance meanwhile extended its activities from intelligence-gathering and propaganda to extensive acts of sabotage against railways and factories. Acknowledging the leadership of General de Gaulle, the movement offered a basis for the assertion of an anti-Vichy French patriotism.

A derailment caused by the French Resistance, c. 1942.

Preparing the Normandy invasion

The Western Allies planned a cross-Channel invasion of France for May 1944, later shifted to June. Eisenhower was in charge of the operation, codenamed Overlord, with Montgomery commanding Allied land forces. With 1.5 million US soldiers stationed in Britain, the Germans knew an invasion was coming, but not where or when. A deception plan, involving dummy vehicles and fake radio traffic, encouraged the Germans to believe the Allies would land at the Pas de Calais, but Rommel, commanding Atlantic Wall fortifications on the French coast, identified Normandy as a likely target and reinforced its defences. Through spring 1944 Allied bombers carried out extensive attacks upon road and rail links across northern France, aided by saboteurs of the French Resistance. Specialist equipment was developed for the landings, including Mulberry floating harbours and 'funny' tanks to operate on the beaches. Troops practised large-scale seaborne landings. One rehearsal, at Slapton, Devon, was surprised by German naval attack craft in April, leading to the loss of almost 800 lives. It was a stiff reminder of how hazardous the whole operation remained.

American troops land on a beach in England during a rehearsal for the invasion of Nazi-occupied France.

The D-Day landings

Planned for 5th June 1944, to take advantage of moonlight and suitable tides, the Normandy landings were almost cancelled because of bad weather. Gambling on a brief respite, Eisenhower gave the go-ahead for 6th June. During the night airborne forces landed by glider and parachute inland from the invasion beaches, while 130,000 American, British, Canadian, Polish and French soldiers sailed across the Channel. A massive bombardment by naval guns pummelled German fortifications at dawn as the landing craft headed ashore in their five sectors, code-named Omaha, Utah, Gold, Juno and Sword. The operation did not go smoothly. Because of poor weather the airborne forces were widely scattered. Many landing craft also came ashore in the wrong places. Clearing obstacles on the beaches under fire caused delays and casualties. Amphibious tanks sank in choppy surf. At Omaha beach, American troops stayed pinned down near the water's edge into the afternoon. After hard fighting German coastal defences were overcome and the landing beaches secured, at a cost of around 10,000 Allied casualties.

Bird's-eye view of landing craft, barrage balloons and Allied troops landing in Normandy. The D-Day landings remain the largest seaborne invasion in history.

General Eisenhower

Dwight D Eisenhower, known affectionately as 'Ike', was an unlikely choice to command the US army in the European theatre in 1942. His military career up to that point had been solid rather than spectacular and he had no combat experience at all. However, US Chief of Staff General George Marshall perceived in him a cool head, a talent for planning and the diplomatic skills necessary for conducting a war as part of an alliance. Eisenhower presided over the Torch landings in North Africa and subsequent Allied landings in Sicily and mainland Italy before being appointed commander of Supreme Headquarters Allied Expeditionary Force (SHAEF) for the invasion of Normandy. His decision to go ahead with the landings on 6th June 1944 in the face of doubtful weather conditions was an impressive example of responsible judgment. While some US generals exhibited discourtesy towards the British, Eisenhower worked hard to calm tempers and to hold the alliance together. His leadership contributed vitally to the defeat of Germany and he later had a distinguished political career, serving as US president from 1953–61.

The Battle of Normandy

A week after D-Day the Allied forces in Normandy had joined up to form a single beachhead, but key objectives had not been taken. The Germans did not have the strength to overrun the Allies, but nor were the Allies able to achieve a decisive breakout in terrain of hills, woods and fields (the 'bocage') that favoured the defence. The Americans took Cherbourg on 27th June, but its port facilities had been destroyed. The British and Canadians laboured in front of Caen, which was not taken until mid-July, by which time British bombing had flattened the city. Frustration led to furious rows between US commanders and Montgomery.

Eventually the Germans cracked. At the start of August the Americans captured Avranches and spread out into Brittany and south to the Loire. German forces were trapped between the British and Canadians advancing from Caen and the Americans to the south. Some escaped through a narrow gap at Falaise, but the devastation of German armoured forces, chiefly by air attack, was immense. By 20th August the Battle of Normandy was over.

Bocage country at Cotentin peninsula, northern France.

The Oradour-sur-Glane Massacre

The Allied landings in Normandy on 6th June 1944 triggered an outbreak of armed activity by the French Resistance and ruthless German operations to suppress it. The Waffen SS 2nd Panzer Division, stationed in southwest France, reacted with exceptional brutality. On 9th June, after fighting in the Corrèze region, the SS hanged 99 men in reprisals at Tulle.

The following day elements of the division entered the village of Oradour-sur-Glane in the Haute-Vienne region. In response to a report that the Resistance had captured a German officer in a neighbouring village, the SS decided to massacre the entire population. The men were taken into farm buildings, machine-gunned and incinerated. The women and children were locked in the village church, which was then set on fire. Those who attempted to escape the burning building were shot. In total 190 men, 247 women and 205 children were killed. Many of the SS soldiers who carried out the massacre subsequently died in the fighting in Normandy.

The village of Oradour-sur-Glane has been preserved in its devastated state as a monument to the horrors of the war.

Fighting in southern France

Renamed the French Forces of the Interior (FFI), in a vain attempt to win German recognition for their status as soldiers, the Resistance in southern France attempted armed insurrection in 1944. The most notable uprising occurred in the mountainous Vercors region, in the foothills of the Alps, where the 'maquisards' Resistance fighters declared the Free Republic of Vercors on 3rd July. The Germans responded by sending in substantial forces, including an airborne assault in gliders on 21st July. The maquisards were overwhelmed and a series of massacres followed, notably at Vassieux-en-Vercors. On 15th August Allied forces began an invasion of southern France, Operation Dragoon. Some 150,000 chiefly US and Free French troops landed at beaches west of Nice, meeting limited opposition. They enjoyed support from the FFI, which is reckoned to have fielded some 75,000 fighters. Free French Forces under General Jean de Lattre de Tassigny, aided by the FFI, captured Toulon on 27th August and Marseilles two days later. Within four weeks of the Normandy landings, most of southern France had been liberated.

Vassieux-en-Vercors, France, and the cemetery in which victims of the July 1944 German massacre are buried.

The liberation of Paris

After the Allied victory in Normandy, Patton's US Third Army, exploring south and eastwards, crossed the Seine River on 23rd August 1944. Eisenhower had not intended to order a drive towards Paris, preferring to bypass the French capital. However, the Free French were determined to liberate the city, where Resistance groups had risen in armed insurrection and were fighting the Germans in the streets. After de Gaulle threatened to take independent action, Eisenhower authorized General Philippe Leclerc's French Second Armoured Division, part of Third Army, to head for Paris with US infantry support. On 24th August the French were held up by stiff German opposition, but in the night some of Leclerc's tanks found their way into the middle of the city and parked outside the Hotel de Ville. The following day German military governor General Dietrich von Choltitz, ignoring an order from Hitler to devastate Paris, surrendered after instructing his troops to withdraw from the city. On 26th August de Gaulle led a French victory parade down the Champs Elysées, which was followed by an American parade three days later.

Crowds of French patriots line the Champs Elysées to view their liberators passing through the Arc de Triomphe. Paris, 26th August 1944.

Rebuilding France

When they invaded France, the Allies intended to place liberated areas under their own military government. However, determined to re-establish France as an independent power, de Gaulle appointed his own representatives to take over local administration as the armies advanced and, once installed in Paris, set up a provisional government that included socialists and communists as well as his own followers. The Vichy government, withdrawn to Germany, had lost all credibility. Inevitably there was a settling of scores with collaborators. In areas under Gaullist control retribution was meted out by tribunals. Elsewhere, especially where communist-led Resistance groups were in the ascendant, thousands of alleged collaborators were summarily executed. Many were guilty of crimes, but others were victims of class justice or personal vendettas. The number of people killed in this 'cleansing' of France may have totalled 50,000. It was de Gaulle's achievement to bring a semblance of unity to this profoundly divided country and win recognition for France as one of the victorious Allies.

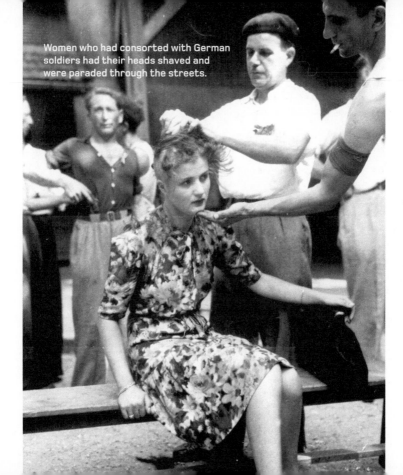

Women who had consorted with German soldiers had their heads shaved and were paraded through the streets.

The failed assassination of Hitler

As early as 1938 some German army officers began plotting to overthrow Hitler, fearing his rule would lead to a disastrous war. Germany's early victories in World War II dampened opposition, but the worsening military situation from 1943 revived the conspiracy. The plotters, who included some civil servants as well as army officers, intended to assassinate the Führer, seize power from the Nazis and negotiate a compromise peace with the Western Allies. After a number of botched attempts, the task was entrusted to an officer who had been wounded in Tunisia in 1943, Colonel Claus von Stauffenberg. On 20th July 1944, von Stauffenberg flew to Hitler's headquarters at Rastenberg in East Prussia for a conference and left a bomb in a briefcase under a table where the Führer was sitting. The bomb exploded, wrecking the room, but remarkably Hitler emerged unscathed. His revenge on the plotters was thorough and brutal. Von Stauffenberg was shot; hundreds of others were tortured and hanged. Field Marshals Erwin Rommel and Günther von Kluge, loosely implicated in the plot, were allowed to commit suicide.

Mussolini is shown the destroyed interior of Hitler's headquarters.

V-1 flying bombs

Apparently facing certain defeat, Hitler placed his hopes in two possibilities – either that the Western Allies would turn against the Soviet Union, or that a 'miracle weapon' would change the course of the war. At Peenemünde on the Baltic, German researchers worked on V-weapons (*Vergeltungswaffen*, or 'revenge weapons') to strike at Britain. On 13th June 1944, a week after the D-Day landings, the first V-1 flying bombs were launched from sites in northern France against southeast England.

The V-1 was a pilotless aeroplane driven by a primitive jet engine and packed with explosives. Thousands struck London by day and night, causing heavy casualties and widespread damage to buildings, and provoking a mass evacuation. Flying at around 640 kmh (400 mph), the V-1s could be intercepted by anti-aircraft fire or the fastest Allied fighters, but they remained a potent threat to London until mid-October when their launch sites were overrun by Allied forces.

A V-1 flies over suburban London. Limited attacks on England continued into 1945 with V-1s air-launched from Heinkel He-111 bombers. The flying bombs were also extensively used against the Belgian port of Antwerp.

The V-2 rocket

The world's first ballistic missile, the V-2 rocket had more potential than the V-1 flying bomb to be the 'miracle weapon' Hitler needed. It was the brainchild of Wernher von Braun, an engineer who began working on rocket engines in the 1930s. He achieved the first launch of the A-4 rocket at Peenemünde in 1942 but production was delayed by RAF bombing of the site in August 1943. Rebranded the V-2 it finally entered service in September 1944, employed chiefly against London and Antwerp.

Travelling at supersonic speed, the V-2 gave no warning of its approach and could not be intercepted. However, the Germans had no means of knowing where the rockets landed and, as a result of a British deception plan, many were wrongly targeted to fall in the country. Manufactured by slave labour at an underground factory, V-2s were only produced in limited numbers. In London they killed about 2,700 people, compared with almost 6,000 killed by V-1s. Surrendering to the Americans at the war's end, von Braun later proved vital to the US missile and space programmes.

A V-2 rocket on display at the Peenemünde Army Research Centre.

Operation Bagration

In 1944 the Soviet Red Army continued the great advances begun in 1943, lifting the Siege of Leningrad in January and taking Sebastopol in Crimea the following May. On 23rd June, almost exactly three years after Hitler's invasion of the Soviet Union, the Soviets launched Operation Bagration, a vast offensive on a 700-km (450-mile) wide front. Thrusting into Belarus and the Baltic states with 1.7 million soldiers and 2,700 tanks, they overwhelmed German forces inferior in numbers and equipment. Soviet troops occupied Minsk on 3rd July, crossed into Poland and, on 2nd August, reached the outskirts of Warsaw. As the Red Army cleared German troops from Soviet territory and began to advance further westwards, Germany was deserted by its allies. Romania succumbed to Soviet forces in August, Finland signed an armistice in September, and Bulgaria switched sides, becoming a Soviet ally. In October, at a meeting in Moscow, Churchill and Stalin informally agreed that Bulgaria and Romania would come within the Soviet sphere of influence, while Stalin conceded Greece to the West. A new postwar order in Europe was taking shape.

A Katyusha missile launcher on display at the exhibition of Soviet weaponry at the National Museum of the History of the Great Patriotic War, Kiev.

The Warsaw uprising

On 1st August 1944, with Soviet troops approaching Warsaw, the Polish Resistance Home Army launched an uprising against German occupation forces in the city. The Home Army owed allegiance to the anti-Soviet Polish government-in-exile in London and did not wish to owe its liberation to the Red Army. The Soviet Union had its own communist Polish exile government that it intended to install in power. The Home Army, numbering 20,000 fighters and led by General Tadeusz Bor Komorowski, took possession of large areas of the city in the first four days of the insurrection, but the Germans responded by sending in Waffen SS troops with tanks, artillery and air support. The Soviet army halted its advance outside Warsaw and made no attempt to intervene as the revolt was crushed with extreme brutality. The Home Army surrendered on 2nd October, after which the Germans systematically destroyed most of the city's buildings that were still standing. Around 200,000 Poles were killed in the suppression of the uprising. Warsaw was not occupied by the Red Army until it resumed its advance in mid-January 1945.

Home Army soldiers fight during the Warsaw uprising. One man is armed with a Błyskawica machine pistol.

Resistance in Greece and Yugoslavia

The fraught politics of 'liberation' in the final phase of the war were demonstrated in Greece and Yugoslavia, both countries with substantial armed Resistance movements. In Greece the largest partisan group was the communist-led ELAS, which was hostile to the monarchist Resistance, EDES. When the Germans withdrew from Greece in October 1944, Britain intervened militarily to restore a monarchist government under King George II. The communist partisans were temporarily defeated and disarmed, but civil war followed from 1946.

In Yugoslavia resistance was split between Josip Broz Tito's communist-led partisans and Draza Mihailovic's pro-monarchist Chetniks. The Allies supported Tito, because he was keener to fight the Germans. Tito's partisans grew to 800,000 strong and were considered the most militarily effective of all Resistance movements. The partisans joined with the Soviets in driving the Germans out of the Yugoslav capital Belgrade in October 1944. Postwar, Tito ruled Yugoslavia as a communist state.

Karakolithos National Resistance Memorial, erected in memory of a battle between partisans of the Greek Liberation Army (ELAS) and the Nazis, and the subsequent execution by the Nazis of 134 Greek citizens.

The Allied advance towards Germany

In August 1944 there were expectations that Nazi Germany would be defeated by Christmas. After the breakout from Normandy the Allied forces swept across France and Belgium. British troops liberated Brussels on 3rd September, while the Americans thrust into eastern France, advancing towards the German border. But the Allies' progress eventually ran out of steam because their supply system could not keep pace. German troops clung on to the French Channel ports, so fuel and munitions still had to be brought from Normandy. The Belgian port of Antwerp was captured but could not be used for resupply because the Germans controlled its approaches along the Scheldt estuary. German resistance stiffened. Montgomery's Operation Market Garden, an ambitious attempt to break into Germany through the Netherlands, failed. Further south the Americans ran into the Siegfried Line defences, a network of minefields and fortified strongpoints. In a battle fought in the Hürtgen Forest from September through to December, the Americans suffered over 30,000 casualties. Approaching the year's end, the Allies had ground to a halt.

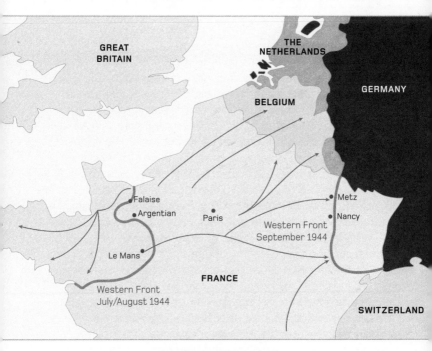

Western Front, 1944

The bridge too far

Commanding Allied forces in Belgium in September 1944, Montgomery devised a risky plan for a thrust across the Netherlands into Germany. Airborne troops were to seize key bridges behind German lines at Eindhoven, Nijmegen and Arnhem. Tanks of British Second Army would advance over the bridges to the German border north of the Ruhr. Code-named Market Garden, the operation began on 17th September. Some 20,000 airborne troops in 1,500 transport aircraft and 500 gliders took off from England. US 101st Airborne at Eindhoven captured most of its objectives and the British tanks reached them the following day. At Nijmegen, however, US 82nd Airborne encountered tough German opposition and the key bridge was not seized until 20th September. The delay placed British 1st Airborne, tasked with holding the Rhine bridge at Arnhem, in a perilous position. Because of errors in the landings, only one parachute battalion reached the bridge. Counter-attacked by two Waffen-SS Panzer divisions they surrendered on 21st September. The British armoured advance was blocked and the operation abandoned.

Douglas Dakotas drop paratroops of 1st Airborne Brigade at Renkum, west of Arnhem, 17th September 1944.

The Battle of the Bulge

On 16th December 1944 Hitler launched a surprise counter-offensive on the Western Front. In a plan similar to his successful attack on France in May 1940, he advanced armoured forces through the forested Ardennes, intending to sweep northwards to Antwerp, forcing the British to evacuate their forces from Belgium in a second Dunkirk. As overcast winter weather kept Allied aircraft grounded, the Germans broke through the US lines spreading chaos and confusion. Their advance was delayed by stout resistance at key points, notably Bastogne, where US 101st Airborne Division held out under siege. The German advance created a 'bulge' that was to give the battle its name. Patton's Third Army, attacking the flank of the 'bulge' from the south, relieved Bastogne on 26th December, by which time improving weather had brought Allied air power into play. The Luftwaffe lost 270 aircraft in desperate counter-attacks on Allied airfields and German tanks began to run out of fuel. Petering out by late January 1945, the battle had cost the United States 80,000 casualties, but Hitler's last gamble had failed.

American infantrymen of the 290th Regiment fight in fresh snowfall near Amonines, Belgium.

The Yalta Conference

Stalin, Roosevelt and Churchill met at Yalta on the Black Sea from 4th–11th February 1945, to discuss the imminent defeat of Germany. They confirmed plans to divide Germany and Berlin into military occupation zones. The Western Allies accepted Stalin's proposal to 'shift' Poland westward, the Soviet Union keeping the eastern part of the country but compensating the Poles with territory taken from Germany. Stalin offered fine words about democracy and agreed to join the United Nations. He also agreed – crucially from Roosevelt's point of view – to join in the war against Japan once Germany was beaten.

The conference was later denounced by critics as the occasion on which Eastern Europe was abandoned to communist oppression. However, unless the Western Allies were prepared to fight the Soviet Union, there was no way they could prevent Stalin doing what he liked in the countries his armies had occupied. As Stalin is quoted as saying: 'Everyone imposes his own system as far as his army can reach.'

The 'Big Three' sit on a patio together. This was the last
time the three leaders met, Roosevelt dying on 12th April.

Germany attacked from east and west

In January 1945 the war in Europe entered its endgame. While the Western Allies were finishing off the Battle of the Bulge, the Soviet Union launched a massive offensive in Poland with armies commanded by Zhukov and General Ivan Konev. Deploying more than two million men over a 480-km (300-mile) wide front, by early February they had advanced from the Vistula to the Oder, where they halted to prepare for a final drive on Berlin, only 60 km (40 miles) away. Budapest, the capital of Germany's ally Hungary, fell to the Soviets after prolonged fighting in mid-February and another Soviet army advanced to the Baltic.

The Western Allies resumed their offensive in February and the first US troops established a bridgehead across the Rhine at Remagen on 7th March. Patton's US Third Army crossed the river on 22nd March, stealing some of the thunder from Montgomery's 21st Army Group, which began a large-scale crossing the following day. While generals vied for glory, Eisenhower insisted there would be no race to Berlin, which was left for the Red Army to conquer.

Invading Germany, 1945

→	Western Allied advanced
→	Soviet advanced
—	German front line, 1 Apr
--	German front line, 20 Apr
—	Western Allied front, 7 May
—	Soviet front, 7 May

THE NETHERLANDS

Amsterdam

Hamburg

Hanover

Berlin

Torgau

BELGIUM

GERMANY

Frankfurt

Prague

Krakow

FRANCE

Vienna

Budapest

SWITZERLAND

HUNGARY

Milan

Venice

Genoa

ITALY

YUGOSLAVIA

Germany faces defeat

After the attempted assassination of Hitler in July 1944, the Nazi Party tightened its hold on all aspects of German life. Hitler placed propaganda chief Joseph Goebbels in charge of 'the total deployment of all Germans against the annihilatory will of our Jewish-international enemies'. All males aged from 16 to 60 not already engaged in the war were conscripted into the *Volkssturm*, a poorly armed militia. By February 1945 Germany had lost the war. Production chief Albert Speer announced that German industry could no longer equip the troops. With the German army suffering massive casualties, the *Volkssturm* was deployed futilely in the front line – at least 175,000 were slaughtered. As Allied bombers battered Berlin, Hitler was forced to withdraw to a bunker under the Reich Chancellery garden. His refusal to surrender was absolute. Most Germans had long lost faith in their Führer. His last radio broadcast on 31st January was greeted with widespread scepticism. But the German people fought on with blind desperation amid their ruined cities, feeling they had no alternative.

Hitler shakes hands with a 12-year-old Hitler Youth soldier in the last-known Associated Press photograph of the Führer to be taken before his suicide.

Soviet atrocities and German refugees

From October 1944, when Red Army troops first occupied German villages in East Prussia, the Soviets committed numerous atrocities against German civilians. Killing, rape and looting were sometimes encouraged and almost always tolerated by Soviet officers. The troops had witnessed the results of the appalling massacres carried out by the Nazi invaders in the Soviet Union and felt justified in exacting revenge.

The Soviet atrocities were publicized by the Nazi government, as it attempted to organize a general withdrawal of all ethnic Germans from territory in the Soviet line of advance. Both organized and spontaneous flight brought millions of German refugees streaming westwards by early 1945. More than one million were evacuated by sea across the Baltic. In total about 600,000 people are thought to have died of hardship and military action while fleeing to the West. Fear of the grim consequences of Soviet conquest encouraged Germans to fight to the death.

Among the Soviet atrocities was the sinking of the transport ship *Wilhelm Gustloff*, pictured here at Gdansk (Danzig). It was sunk by a Soviet submarine on 30th January, drowning 9,400 refugees from Prussia and the Baltic states.

Liberating the camps

As soon as it became clear that Germany was likely to lose the war, the Nazis began trying to hide the evidence of their crimes. The death camps at Treblinka, Sobibor and Belzec, where more than one million people had been murdered, were obliterated, the gas chambers destroyed and the land ploughed over. However, in July 1944 the Soviets overran the Majdanek extermination camp, finding ample evidence of the mass killings that had taken place there. In January 1945 they reached Auschwitz, which had been left intact but emptied of most of its surviving prisoners, moved westwards in a brutal death march.

Those prisoners from Auschwitz who survived the march ended up in camps inside Germany, such as Bergen-Belsen and Buchenwald. Thousands more died of starvation and disease before the armies of the Western Allies liberated the camps in the final stage of the war. Shown in cinema newsreels, images of the heaped corpses and skeleton-like prisoners at Belsen were the most persuasive evidence that the war to overthrow the Nazi regime had been just.

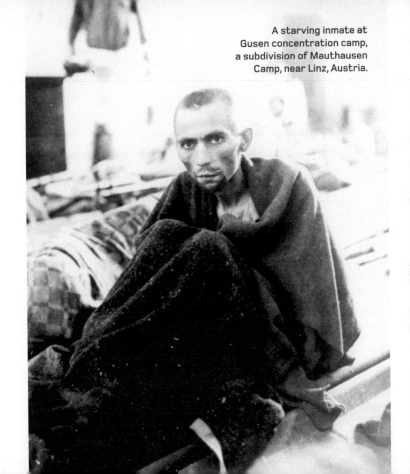

A starving inmate at Gusen concentration camp, a subdivision of Mauthausen Camp, near Linz, Austria.

The death of Mussolini

By 1945 Mussolini was an almost powerless figure, his Italian Social Republic in northern Italy largely disregarded by the country's German occupiers. Through the first three months of the year the military situation in Italy remained static, but the Allies resumed their offensive in April. US Fifth Army thrust north from Bologna into the Po Valley and on towards Milan, while British Eighth Army advanced up the east coast to Venice. The Germans retreated in increasing disarray, harassed by Italian partisans who were active throughout northern Italy. Amid the general collapse, on 25th April Mussolini and his entourage fled, hoping to reach Switzerland and then fly to Spain. They were intercepted by communist partisans near Lake Como and summarily executed by firing squad on 28th April. The bodies of Mussolini and his mistress Clara Petacci were taken to Milan and exhibited hanging upside down at a service station. General Heinrich von Vietinghoff, who had succeeded Kesselring as German commander in Italy, sought an armistice on 29th April. Eighth Army occupied Trieste on 2nd May, as the armistice came into effect.

Hitler's suicide

On 16th April 1945 Soviet generals Zhukov and Konev launched the final drive to capture Berlin, with half a million men under their command. On every front German forces were collapsing – Vienna had fallen to the Red Army, the Americans had encircled 300,000 German troops in the Ruhr, the British were advancing on Bremen. Nonetheless, German resistance to the Soviet offensive was fierce. Zhukov's initial attack on the Seelow Heights cost 30,000 lives. Berlin came under artillery fire on 20th April, Hitler's 56th birthday. By 26th April Soviet forces were fighting in the streets, opposed by the SS, Hitler Youth and *Volkssturm*. As the Red Army closed in on his bunker, Hitler conducted the last rites of his regime. He wrote a final testament, blaming the German people for his defeat and proclaiming the destruction of the Jews his supreme achievement. On 30th April he committed suicide with his companion Eva Braun, whom he had married the previous day. Goebbels and his wife also killed themselves, along with their six children, before the fighting in Berlin ceased on 2nd May.

Raising the Soviet flag over the Reichstag, Berlin.

The German surrenders and VE Day

On 25th April 1945 American and Soviet troops advancing across Germany met amicably at Torgau on the Elbe River. By that point the chief aim of most Germans was, if possible, to end up in the hands of the Western Allies rather than the Soviets. After Hitler's death at the end of April, his successor Admiral Karl Dönitz temporized, still seeking some way to surrender to the West alone. Meanwhile, a series of local German surrenders took place. The armies in Italy and in Berlin lay down their arms on 2nd May. Two days later forces in northwest Germany surrendered to Montgomery on Lüneberg Heath. On 7th May Dönitz sent General Alfred Jodl to Eisenhower's headquarters in Reims to sign a general surrender, but Eisenhower insisted the ceremony be repeated in Berlin on 8th May, with Zhukov taking the surrender on behalf of the Soviet Union. This was declared Victory in Europe (VE) Day and wild celebrations erupted in the cities of the victorious powers, muted only by the recognition that the war against Japan remained to be won.

Crowds gather in London's Trafalgar Square,
to celebrate the Allied victory in Europe, 1945.

Island-hopping in the Pacific

In 1943 American strength in the Pacific grew to a point where a major offensive could be launched against Japan's far-flung defensive perimeter. The action proceeded on two fronts. In the Southwest Pacific, MacArthur conducted an army-led push towards the Philippines. In the Central Pacific, Nimitz sent the navy and Marines on a drive towards the Marianas.

The Central Pacific offensive began in November with landings on Japanese-held Makin and Tarawa atolls in the Gilbert Islands. The seizure of Kwajalein and Eniwetok in the Marshalls followed in early 1944. A pattern was immediately established. American strength in carriers, landing craft and amphibious vehicles ensured the islands could be taken, but small numbers of Japanese defenders, fighting to the death, imposed disproportionate losses on US troops – 3,000 casualties at Tarawa alone. The devastation of the Japanese naval base at Truk in the Carolinas by carrier aircraft in February and April confirmed Japan's defensive perimeter was disintegrating, exposing the Japanese homeland to risk of attack.

Three Marines crawl towards a Japanese dugout to knock out snipers during battles on Eniwetok atoll in the Marshall Islands, while a US plane flies overhead, 1944.

The battle for Saipan

US Marines began landings on Saipan in the Marshall Islands on 15th June 1944. The Marshalls represented a vital step in American progress, as they would provide secure airbases from which B-29 bombers could strike the Japanese homeland. Saipan was garrisoned by about 30,000 Japanese troops under General Yoshitsugu Saito, and had a population of around 25,000. Despite fierce resistance the Marines established a beachhead and landings by US army infantry followed two days later. The Japanese withdrew to fight in the mountainous interior, where American progress was slow. Flamethrowers were used extensively to clear the Japanese out of caves. On 7th July, pinned down in the north, Saito ordered a suicidal 'banzai' charge by his remaining troops, including the wounded, inflicting substantial American casualties. Japanese civilians were encouraged to commit suicide, which many did by jumping off cliffs. About 29,000 Japanese soldiers and possibly 15,000 civilians died before fighting ceased on 9th July. The Americans had suffered 3,000 killed and more than 10,000 wounded out of 70,000 troops committed.

Marine infantrymen move fast to take up positions in Garapan, the principal city of Saipan.

The Battle of the Philippine Sea

During the landings on Saipan in the Marianas in June 1944, Japanese Imperial Navy commanders planned an attack on the US naval forces in the Philippine Sea supporting the landings. They hoped to gain a crucial advantage by trapping the US fleet between a Japanese carrier force at sea and air bases on the islands. They failed to realize that the US navy's carrier fleet had made vital progress since the start of the war, with better aircraft, more experienced pilots, and superior tactics based on radar. The quality of Japanese naval aviation, in contrast, had declined through loss of experienced pilots and static technology.

On 19th June waves of Japanese carrier aircraft flying in to attack the US fleet were slaughtered by US Grumman Hellcat fighters. More than 300 Japanese aircraft were shot down for few losses of American pilots, who cruelly dubbed the engagement 'the Marianas Turkey Shoot'. On this, and the following day, the Japanese also lost three carriers to air or submarine attack. Their carrier fleet ceased to exist as an effective fighting force.

Grumman Hellcat fighters in flight over Luzon, Philippines, September 1944.

The Battle of Leyte Gulf

After US forces completed their occupation of the Marianas, taking Guam and Tinian in July-August 1944, General MacArthur mounted his promised return to the Philippines. On 20th October two US army corps began landings on Leyte Island in the central Philippines, precipitating probably the largest naval battle in history. Seeing the invasion as a last chance to inflict a decisive defeat on the US navy, the Japanese dispatched a formidable fleet led by nine battleships and 19 cruisers. They were to attack in a pincer movement around Leyte and Samar islands while Japanese carriers – no longer with aircraft on board – lured US carriers away to the north. This distraction worked and there was a dangerous moment when Japanese capital ships surprised the US escort carriers and destroyers covering the landings. But overall the battle was a catastrophe for Japan. Three Japanese battleships were sunk, including *Musashi*, one of the heaviest, most powerfully armed warships ever built. More than half the Japanese cruisers were also lost. The Imperial Navy would never again attempt to challenge American command of the sea.

General Douglas MacArthur wades ashore during initial landings at Leyte, Philippine Islands.

The Japanese Ichi-Go offensive

The war in the Pacific had turned the Chinese theatre into something of a backwater. However, in April 1944 Japanese troops launched Operation Ichi-Go, a large-scale offensive against territory held by Chiang Kai-shek's Chinese Nationalists. Their main objective was to capture airfields that had been used by the Americans to mount bombing raids on Japanese-held Formosa (Taiwan) and that, from June 1944, would provide bases for B-29 bombers attacking southern Japan. Employing half a million soldiers, the Japanese occupied Hunan, Guangxi and Guizhou provinces in fighting that lasted into December. Their advance overran the airfields, although the American capture of the Marianas, within bombing range of Japan, made this loss less significant. The Chinese defeats left the Americans angered by the inertia and corruption of the Nationalists, who had made poor use of US military supplies. They unsuccessfully proposed placing US General Joseph Stilwell in charge of the Nationalist forces and even considered shifting their military aid to the Chinese Communists.

Chinese soldiers help civilians evacuate Liuchow ahead of the advancing Japanese army. The site of an airfield used by Nationalist Chinese and US army air forces, it was captured by the Japanese in November 1944.

Iwo Jima

In February 1945, while several hundred thousand US troops were engaged in savage fighting for control of Luzon in the Philippine campaign, attention was focused on an attack on a tiny volcanic rock called Iwo Jima. In the Pacific about 10,500 km (650 miles) southeast of Tokyo, Iwo Jima had no great strategic significance, although it was thought of some use to the US bombing campaign. Under the command of General Tadamichi Kuribayashi, the island's 20,000-strong garrison occupied thoroughly prepared defences. Their system of bunkers and tunnels survived a preparatory air and sea bombardment. When US Marines went ashore on 19th February they were initially pinned down on crowded beaches under infantry and artillery fire. Fighting inland, the Marines were able to raise the Stars and Stripes on the summit of Mount Suribachi on 23rd February, but it took a further month to subdue Japanese resistance, with 60,000 Marines committed to the fighting. About 26,000 Americans were killed or wounded in the battle. Only 216 Japanese soldiers were taken prisoner. A few others may have survived hidden in caves and tunnels.

Raising the flag on Iwo Jima,
23rd February 1945.

The battle for Okinawa

By spring 1945 US commanders were already planning an invasion of the Japanese mainland, scheduled for November. As a preparatory move they decided to occupy the large island of Okinawa, between Japan and Taiwan. Some 180,000 US Marines and army soldiers began the landings on 1st April. Supported by a vast Allied fleet the troops went ashore almost unopposed, the Japanese concentrating their defences in a heavily fortified mountainous region of the interior. Some of the most ferocious fighting of the entire war took place here over the following three months. Attacked by kamikaze pilots using suicide tactics, the Allied fleet suffered substantial losses. In a last defiant gesture by the Japanese Imperial Navy, the mighty battleship *Yamato* headed for Okinawa and was destroyed by a mass US air attack. On land the death toll among civilians was appalling, with possibly half of the island's 300,000 population killed. By the time the fighting stopped on 22nd June victory had cost the Americans some 50,000 casualties. It was a chilling foretaste of the losses an invasion of the Japanese mainland would entail.

A kamikaze attack on the USS *Missouri*.

Japanese kamikaze pilots

Japanese naval pilots began systematically employing suicide tactics during the battle of Leyte Gulf in October 1944 as a practical response to the overwhelming superiority achieved by American aviation. Facing the near certainty of death in any case, Japanese fliers could at least die inflicting damage on the enemy by using their aircraft as piloted bombs crashing on to warships. The first US vessel sunk by a kamikaze strike was the carrier *St Lo* on 25th October. The special suicide units were dubbed *kamikaze* (divine wind) and rituals were instituted to give their self-sacrifice an aura of sanctity. But suicide pilots soon ceased to be an elite. By 1945 barely trained youngsters were being used to carry out the attacks escorted by experienced pilots. During the Okinawa operation hundreds of kamikaze aircraft based on Japan's Kyushu island struck the Allied fleet in mass attacks known as *kikusui* (floating chrysanthemum). In total kamikaze strikes sank around 50 Allied ships and damaged hundreds more, an astonishing achievement but one that eroded Japanese air power and cost thousands of young Japanese lives.

Members of 72nd Shinbu Squadron. Three of the five are 17 years old and the other two are 18 and 19. The photo was taken the day before their mission.

America bombs Japanese cities

The American strategic bombing campaign against Japan began in June 1944, employing the new B-29 Superfortress long-range bomber flying from airfields in southwest China. The raids had limited effect, however, even after the bombers transferred to bases in the Marianas in October. Flying at high altitude the aircraft encountered the powerful Siberian jet stream, which tended to blow them off course so that few found their targets. Although the raids were conducted in daylight, frequent cloud cover made accurate bomb-aiming impossible. In spring 1945 Bomber Commander General Curtis LeMay changed tactics. The aircraft were to attack Japanese cities by night flying at low altitude, using incendiary bombs instead of high explosives. On the night of 9th-10th March a raid by 279 B-29s caused a firestorm in Tokyo that destroyed one-quarter of the city and killed at least 100,000 people. A succession of similar raids on other Japanese cities followed. Civilians fled to the countryside and industrial output plummeted. By June so much of Tokyo had burned down the Americans considered it no longer worth bombing.

A Boeing Superfortress bombardment group, on an incendiary mission to Osaka, Japan, 1st June 1945.

Japanese balloon bombs

As their cities came under attack from B-29 bombers, the Japanese devised a scheme for bombarding North America with balloon bombs. Their meteorologists had identified the jet stream that, in winter months, could carry hydrogen-filled balloons at high altitude across the Pacific in three days, each loaded with incendiary and high-explosive devices.

Between November 1944 and March 1945, some 9,000 Fu-Go balloons were launched, of which probably 10 per cent reached Canada or the United States. They caused the Allies some consternation and aircraft were deployed to intercept them, but their only significant effect was to kill six civilians in Oregon out for a picnic – the only deaths on the mainland United States attributable to enemy action in the entire war. The balloon offensive highlights the huge disparity between America and Japan by the last year of the conflict. The Japanese still had the will to fight but utterly lacked the necessary resources.

The Fu-Go balloon (above) and its bomb load (right). The balloon had a paper sack 10 m (3 ft) in diameter and an automatic control system to keep it at a constant height in flight.

British victory in Burma

In March 1944 the Japanese forces in Burma mounted an offensive against the British in India. Crossing the border into Assam, they surrounded 100,000 soldiers of the British Indian Army at Imphal. Supplied and reinforced by air, the besieged troops held out until a relief force broke through the encirclement in late June. The Japanese troops withdrew into Burma having suffered over 50,000 casualties. Short of food and decimated by disease, they were pursued by British and Indian forces under General William Slim. Meanwhile, in an operation planned by US General Stilwell, Chinese Nationalist troops cleared the Japanese from northeast Burma.

After Slim's forces captured Mandalay in March 1945, despite stiff resistance, the tide of war had turned against the Japanese. Burmese anti-colonialists, who had welcomed the Japanese as liberators in 1942, now changed sides, their Burma National Army aiding the British. After staging landings on the Burmese coast, the British seized the vital port city of Rangoon in early May.

At Imphal, a Sikh signaller operates a walkie-talkie so that British officers can listen to patrols reporting on Japanese positions. Fighting in Burma continued to the end of the war, to no clear strategic purpose.

Japan's government divided

By summer 1945 Japan's situation was hopeless. Its cities were being destroyed by bombing, its population faced starvation as an Allied naval blockade cut off food imports, and its war machine was running out of fuel. The loss of Okinawa in June was obviously the prelude to an invasion of Japan itself. In the face of these disasters, the Japanese government was paralyzed by internal dissensions. General Tojo had resigned as prime minister after the fall of Saipan in 1944. His successors lacked authority. The Supreme War Council, which took crucial decisions, was evenly split between a 'peace' and a 'war' party. The peace faction, enjoying the qualified approval of the emperor, favoured a negotiated end to the war, though attaching conditions that in practice made a deal improbable. The war party, which had powerful support among army officers, sought a fight to the death, believing a suicidal defence of the homeland would preserve the Japanese spirit. Various peace feelers were put out unofficially, but no formal attempt to negotiate a surrender was possible given the virulent opposition of the war faction.

Japanese Emperor Hirohito in the later months of the war.

The Manhattan Project

In December 1941 President Roosevelt launched a secret programme, code-named the Manhattan Project, to produce an atom bomb. Scientists in all countries knew such a bomb was theoretically possible, but in 1941 they were far from knowing how it might actually work. Most progress had been achieved by scientists in Britain, chiefly Jewish refugees from Nazi Germany. The British handed this research to the Americans, who alone had the resources to make the atom bomb a reality. The Manhattan Project was not only a scientific effort, executed by researchers in Chicago and at Los Alamos in New Mexico, but also a vast industrial programme employing 200,000 people in factories across the United States. It cost the US government $2 billion, funding allocated without authorization from Congress. Very few people knew of the project's existence, even in the US government and military leadership. The bomb was intended for use against Germany, but at an Anglo-American summit meeting in Quebec in September 1944 it was agreed that, if Germany had been defeated, the bomb would be dropped on Japan.

American physicist and head of the programme, Robert Oppenheimer inspects the atomic test site in the desert at Los Alamos, 1945.

The first atom bomb test

The surrender of Germany in May 1945 made some scientists engaged in the Manhattan Project query the use of the atom bomb. A document known as the Franck Report, after scientist James Franck, suggested America renounce dropping the bomb on Japan. But this was a minority opinion, even among scientists, and was not taken seriously by the US government. A presidential committee set up to advise on the bomb unanimously agreed its use without warning. Another committee coolly debated which Japanese cities to target. Meanwhile, General Leslie Groves, in overall command of the project, organized and trained a squadron of B-29s to drop the bomb. The scientists at Los Alamos developed two types of atom bomb, the uranium-based 'Little Boy' and the plutonium-based 'Fat Man'. They were sure Little Boy would work but Fat Man was more problematic, so Robert Oppenheimer organized a test of the plutonium device at Alamogordo in the New Mexico desert on 16th July. The result exceeded expectations, the explosion generating heat and light of an intensity never before seen on Earth.

The 'jumbo' container being positioned for testing the first atom bomb at Alamogordo, New Mexico, 1945.

The Potsdam Conference

On 17th July 1945, the day after the first atom bomb test, Allied leaders met for the final summit conference of the war at Potsdam in Berlin. During the meeting, Churchill, defeated in a general election, was replaced by Clement Attlee. For Harry S Truman, successor to the US presidency on Roosevelt's death, it was his first encounter with Stalin. The president informed the Soviet leader of the successful atom bomb test, believing the new weapon would strengthen America's hand in dealings with the Soviets. Stalin already knew about the bomb from his spies and appeared unimpressed. One of America's chief aims at Potsdam was to induce the Soviet Union to join the war against Japan. This Stalin agreed he would do in August. Privately, Truman hoped the atom bomb might end the war with Japan before the Soviets became involved. The Potsdam Declaration, broadcast on 26th July, called on Japan to surrender unconditionally or face 'prompt and utter destruction' – without specifying how this destruction would occur. Japanese Prime Minister Admiral Kantaro Suzuki disdainfully dismissed the declaration as containing nothing new.

The final meeting at the Potsdam Conference.

The bombing of Hiroshima and Nagasaki

Hiroshima on Honshu island, southern Japan, was selected as a target for the first atom bomb because it was largely untouched by conventional bombing, contained sufficient military facilities to be considered a legitimate target, and was mostly flat, providing an opportunity to demonstrate the full destructive power of the new weapon. The bomb was carried in a B-29 bomber piloted by Colonel Paul Tibbets, who named the aircraft *Enola Gay*.

Taking off from Tinian Island in the Marianas on 6th August 1945, escorted by two other B-29s, *Enola Gay* dropped its bomb at 8.15 local time from high altitude. The city was utterly destroyed. An estimated 140,000 people were killed immediately by heat and blast or died from the effects of nuclear radiation over the following months. Three days later a second atom bomb was dropped. The intended target was the city of Kokura, but bad weather forced pilot Major Charles Sweeney to divert to Nagasaki. The death toll there was lower, perhaps 80,000, because hills sheltered some areas of the city from the bomb's full effects.

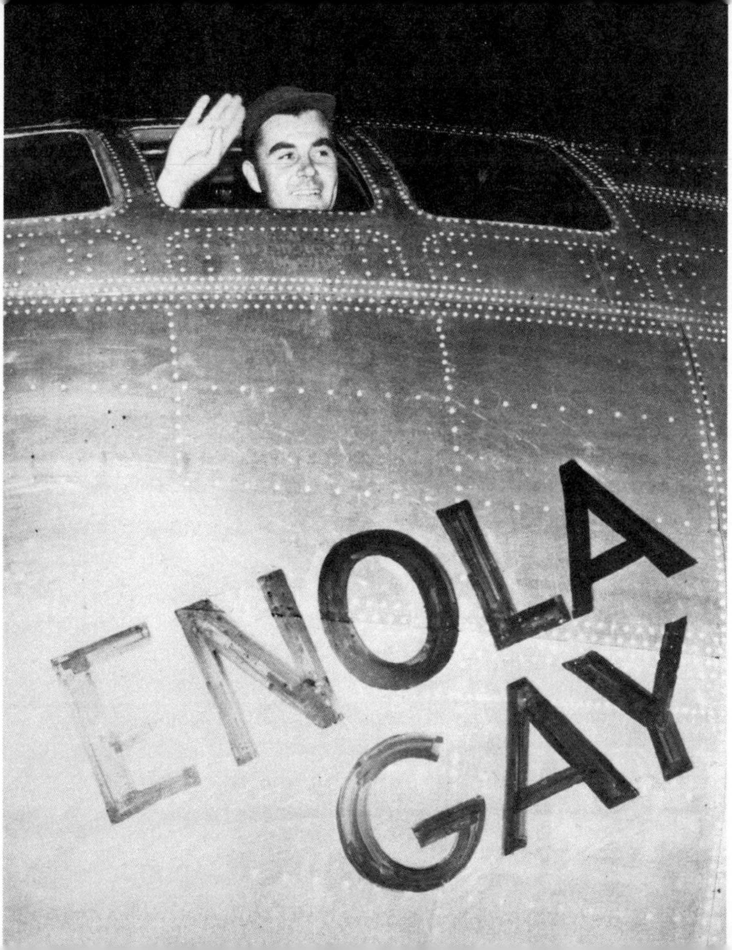
ENOLA
GAY

The Japanese surrender

On 9th August, the day of the Nagasaki bombing, Soviet troops invaded Japanese-occupied Manchuria in overwhelming force. The following day, at a meeting of the Supreme War Council, Emperor Hirohito resolved the political stalemate between 'peace' and 'war' factions by pronouncing in favour of immediate surrender. Japan contacted the United States, offering surrender on the sole condition that the emperor remain on the throne. This condition Truman rejected, stating only that at some future date the Japanese people would be free to choose their own form of government. The American reply reopened the split in the Japanese leadership, but on 14th August the emperor reasserted his determination 'to bear the unbearable'. At the last hour junior army officers attempted a coup to prevent the surrender being broadcast, but loyalty to the emperor generally prevailed. At noon on 15th August the Japanese people were shocked to hear their emperor's voice on the radio, telling them the war had evolved 'not necessarily to Japan's advantage' and the fighting must cease.

The formal Japanese surrender was signed aboard the battleship USS *Missouri* on 2nd September 1945.

Casualties of war

There is no doubt that World War II was more costly in terms of human life than any other conflict in history, but precisely quantifying the losses is impossible. Figures of the total worldwide death toll and for losses in individual countries have been repeatedly revised ever since the war ended, with estimates tending to rise. It was once common to quote 50 million as the total death toll in the conflict worldwide. Now estimates as high as 85 million are considered credible.

The highest proportional loss is believed to have been suffered by Poland, which had about one in six of its population killed, including Polish Jews. The Soviet Union suffered the highest number of military deaths, possibly around ten million, while the German armed services lost about five million men and the Japanese two million. These figures dwarf American military deaths at around 400,000 and the British 350,000. The war was notable for the vast scale of civilian deaths, about one-third of the total. Between three per cent and four per cent of the overall world population died in the conflict.

German women clear up the debris on Berlin's streets. The absence of able-bodied men meant that the responsibility for clearing the wreckage fell mainly to civilian *Trümmerfrauen*, or rubble ladies.

War crimes trials

The victorious Allies were committed to the arrest and trial of Nazi leaders. Some prominent Nazis escaped to South America and SS Chief Heinrich Himmler committed suicide after being arrested. Twenty-one leading figures were tried by a special tribunal in Nuremberg for crimes against peace, war crimes and crimes against humanity. In October 1946 eleven were condemned to death, although Hermann Goering escaped hanging by killing himself in his cell. A similar trial of Japanese leaders in Tokyo led to seven executions, including that of General Tojo.

Many other trials and executions took place, mostly in national courts. In France both Vichy leaders Pétain and Laval were condemned to death, although Pétain's sentence was commuted to life imprisonment. The taste for cleansing soon waned, however, as those implicated in the Nazi or Fascist regimes were found useful by the victors, either for their specialist knowledge or for their readiness to support the new political arrangements favoured by whichever of the Allies was their occupying power.

Defendants in the dock at the Nuremberg Trials: Goering, Hess, von Ribbentrop and Keitel (front row).

Displacement, expulsion and resettlement

After the war 11 million 'displaced persons' (DPs) became the responsibility of the Allied authorities in Germany and Austria and of the newly formed United Nations. They included survivors of Nazi camps, ethnic Germans expelled from central Europe (three million from Poland, two million from Czechoslovakia), and people fleeing persecution by communist regimes. Soviet citizens who had ended up in the West and were 'repatriated' mostly found themselves immediately incarcerated in Stalin's prison camps. Inside the Soviet Union, liberation of territory from German occupation was accompanied by the mass deportation of ethnic minorities deemed guilty of collaboration, notably the Crimean Tatars and the Chechens. Most of the ethnic German refugees were eventually absorbed into West Germany. More than 100,000 anti-communist Poles settled in Britain. Some Jewish survivors found their way to Palestine, contributing to the founding of the state of Israel in 1948. Hundreds of thousands of other DPs lived in camps for years waiting for a country such as Australia, Canada or the United States to accept them as immigrants.

The British ship *Mataroa* brings 1,204 refugees from Nazi persecution to the Haifa port, Palestine (now Israel).

Germany divided

At the end of World War II, Germany and its capital were divided into military occupation zones agreed between the Allies during the war. An Allied Control Council was supposed to coordinate progress towards a more permanent settlement, but the Western Allies and the Soviets were soon locked in acrimonious disagreement over the form a future unified Germany might take. In 1948 the Western powers, frustrated by the lack of progress, decided to introduce a new currency in their three contiguous occupation zones. The Soviets responded by demanding that American, British and French occupation forces leave West Berlin, which was deep within the Soviet zone. When the Western powers refused, the Soviets placed West Berlin under blockade. The Western powers responded by mounting an airlift to supply the Berlin population with food and fuel. The crisis was resolved in 1949. The Soviets abandoned the Berlin blockade, the Western powers recognized a government in West Germany, and the Soviets established a communist regime in East Germany.

British military police erect a sign to mark the division of British and Russian sectors of Berlin, Germany, 1948.

The Iron Curtain

Not only Germany but the whole of Europe was divided after the war. As early as 1946, former British Prime Minister Winston Churchill declared that an 'iron curtain' had descended across the continent, dividing the communist East from the capitalist West. In areas under the control of Stalin's armies, versions of the Soviet social and political system were installed. Czechoslovakia was the last to fall into line after a communist coup in 1948. Only Yugoslavia resisted Stalinism, asserting its own brand of relatively liberal communism.

In Western Europe, versions of liberal democracy mostly prevailed. Communist parties – which in Italy and France had considerable popular support – were excluded from power. In 1949 the North Atlantic Treaty Organization (NATO) was formed, committing the United States to the defence of Western Europe. The admission of West Germany to NATO in 1955 marked a dramatic reversal of the wartime alignment. Europe was to remain a divided continent for four decades.

After the war, America pumped money into Western Europe through the Marshall Plan, promoting an economic recovery that soon opened up a wide gap in living standards between East and West.

Decolonization in Asia

Britain, France and the Netherlands, the major European colonial powers in Asia, emerged from World War II with depleted resources and shattered prestige, while anti-colonial movements had gained strength. In the Dutch East Indies (Indonesia), a liberation movement declared independence from the Netherlands as soon as the Japanese surrendered. The Dutch vainly attempted to reimpose their authority by force before finally accepting Indonesian independence in 1949. The French faced a similar challenge in Vietnam, where the communist-led Viet Minh declared independence in December 1945. France's decision to fight the Viet Minh led them into a disastrous colonial war that ended with defeat at Dien Bien Phu in 1954. The British managed a relatively peaceful withdrawal from the Indian Raj in 1947, although the decision to divide India from Muslim Pakistan left a legacy for future conflict. Burma and Sri Lanka became independent the following year, but in Malaya the British fought to suppress a communist insurgency before leaving in 1957. Britain withdrew its last forces from Singapore in 1971, closing another chapter of history.

President Sukarno (far right), first president of Indonesia.

Postwar Japan and China

In Japan, occupied by the Americans, General MacArthur reconstructed the political system on the British model, which he personally admired. Emperor Hirohito was recast as a constitutional monarch leading a liberal democracy. By the 1950s the US government was welcoming Japan as an ally against communism, and Hiroshima and Nagasaki were flourishing cities again.

In China civil war between Chiang Kai-shek's Nationalists and Mao Zedong's Communists resumed. The Nationalists looked strongest, taking over most of the territory previously occupied by the Japanese, but the morale of Chiang's troops was poor and raging inflation blocked economic recovery. Based at Harbin in Manchuria, in 1947 the Communists began a series of major offensives with conventional forces, rather than guerrilla tactics. By 1949, with his armies disintegrating, Chiang was forced to take refuge in Taiwan. Mao proclaimed a Chinese People's Republic, allied with the Soviet Union.

Crowds in Peking welcome victorious Communist troops following the withdrawal of Nationalist forces from the city, 1949. A portrait of Mao Zedong is among those on display.

The Cold War begins

Only the United States and the Soviet Union emerged from World War II as serious contenders for global leadership. In 1949 the Americans lost their monopoly of nuclear weapons when the Soviets tested their first atom bomb. The following year, communist North Korea invaded pro-American South Korea, triggering large-scale warfare. The United States and its allies intervened militarily under the banner of the United Nations and communist China sent in its army to support North Korea. The fighting ended in stalemate in 1953, by which time America was in the grip of full-blown anti-communist paranoia. Both the United States and the Soviet Union set out to develop more powerful nuclear weapons and more effective delivery systems. The explosion of a hydrogen bomb by the United States in 1954 was followed by the introduction of intercontinental ballistic missiles. Either because of, or in spite of, this nuclear arms race, however, both sides sought to avoid a direct full-scale 'hot war'. The world entered the tense era of the Cold War; a nuclear stalemate based on 'mutually assured destruction'.

US aircraft unload supplies at Tempelhof Airport, Berlin during the Soviet blockade that marked the start of the Cold War.

Recovery and resolution

World War II cast a long shadow. In Britain, financially devastated by the war effort, life remained austere for years, with rationing continuing to 1954 and military conscription to 1960. The Soviet Union did not repatriate its last German prisoner of war until 1956. But from the 1950s economic recovery, at least in the capitalist world, was impressive, especially in the defeated countries, both Japan and West Germany experiencing 'economic miracles'. While economic growth left the ruin and deprivation of World War II a distant memory for prosperous citizens living in their rebuilt cities, the threat of 'World War III' hung permanently in the background. But although wars were fought in which the Americans and Soviets backed opposing sides, either with military supplies or full-scale military intervention, the nuclear arsenals stayed unused. The division of Germany remained the starkest reminder of World War II until reunification in 1990. The last of the military occupation forces of the wartime Allies left Berlin in 1994. By then one of those Allies, the Soviet Union, no longer formally existed. World War II had become history.

The fall of the Berlin Wall, 1991.

Glossary

Allied powers

The countries that fought against Germany and Japan in World War II, including the United States, Britain and its dominions, the Soviet Union, China and France.

Amphibious operations

The combined use of naval and army forces to land troops on coasts or islands.

Area bombing

The indiscriminate bombing of a city without a precise target.

Armistice

An agreement to stop fighting.

Axis powers

The countries that fought against the Allied powers in World War II, chiefly Germany, Italy and Japan.

Baltic States

Collective term used to designate Latvia, Lithuania and Estonia.

Beachhead

An area on an enemy coast or on the far side of a river successfully held by invading troops.

Blitz

The German bombing of London and other British cities in 1940–41 was popularly known as 'the Blitz'.

Blitzkrieg

German military tactics using tanks and motorized infantry supported by aircraft to achieve rapid breakthroughs.

Bolshevik Revolution

The seizure of power by the Bolshevik Party in Russia in 1917, which led to the founding of the communist Soviet Union.

Capital ships

The most important warships in a navy, such as battleships or aircraft carriers.

Collective security

All member states of the League of Nations agreed to join together in military defence of any league member who was a victim of aggression; this was known as 'collective security'.

Colonial empire

Term used for the British, French, Dutch and other European control of peoples in Africa, Asia and the Americas.

Communism

System of government by a single party exercising control over all aspects of life, officially dedicated to world revolution.

Convoy

A system for the defence of merchant shipping in which merchant vessels sail in large groups escorted by naval warships.

Disarmament

Reductions in weapons and the size of armies by international agreement.

Eastern Front

The war fought by Germany in the east, chiefly against the Soviet Union.

Fascism

Originally referring specifically to Benito Mussolini's Fascist movement in Italy, a general term for radical nationalism combining political dictatorship with aggressive militarism.

French Indochina

The area of Southeast Asia under French rule, composed of Vietnam, Cambodia and Laos.

George Cross

A British award for heroism not in battle, often awarded to civilians.

Ghetto

An area in which Jewish people were compelled to live segregated from the non-Jewish population.

Greater Germany

The German Reich as enlarged by Hitler's conquests, including Austria and parts of pre-war Czechoslovakia, Poland and France.

Luftwaffe

The German air force.

Nazi

Short for *Nationalsozialistische Deutsche Arbeiterpartei* (National Socialist German Workers' Party), the ruling party of Hitler's Germany.

National self-determination

The right of people with a sense of ethnic or cultural identity to live under a government of their own choosing, rather than a foreign power.

NKVD

The Soviet People's Commissariat for Internal Affairs, which ran Stalin's secret police organization ruthlessly enforcing communist rule.

Pincer movement

Military manoeuvre in which an army attacks the enemy from both sides, hoping to achieve an encirclement.

Reparations

Payments traditionally made by the loser in a war to compensate the victors for the cost of the conflict.

Rapprochement

In international politics, the establishment of close relations between two previously hostile countries.

Salient

An area that protrudes into enemy-held territory, so that it is surrounded by the enemy on three sides.

Scuttle

To deliberately sink your own warship, usually to prevent it falling into the hands of your enemies.

Scramble

In air warfare, refers to the rapid take-off of aircraft in response to an enemy threat.

Sortie

A brief swift breakout by a naval or army force pinned in a defensive position.

Soviet Union

Officially called the Union of Soviet Socialist Republics (USSR), a communist state that included Russia and Ukraine, with its capital at Moscow.

Western Allies

The United States, Britain and west European members of the Allied powers.

Western Front

The war fought by Germany in the west, chiefly against Britain, France and the United States.

Index

Picture credits

2: National Archives and Records Administration, College Park; 9: National Library of Scotland World War One Official Photos Collection; 11: Library of Congress; 13: Leonard Raven-Hill/Punch; 15: A Bruni/Alinari/Shutterstock; 17: Deutsche Reichsbank; 19: Bundesarchiv, Bild 102-00344A / Heinrich Hoffmann / CC-BY-SA 3.0; 21: Cci/Shutterstock; 23: National Archives and Records Administration, College Park; 25: Universal History Archive/ Shutterstock; 27: Granger/REX/Shutterstock; 29: Juan Guzman; 31: Bundesarchiv, Bild 183-H25224 / Unknown / CC-BY-SA 3.0; 35: Glasshouse Images/Shutterstock; 37: National Archives and Records Administration, College Park; 41: Bundesarchiv, Bild 183-1987-0922-500 / CC-BY-SA 3.0; 43: Granger/Shutterstock; 45: Granger/Shutterstock; 47: National Archives and Records Administration, College Park; 49: National Archives and Records Administration, College Park; 51: Daily Mail /Shutterstock; 55: © Illustrated London News Ltd/Mary Evans Picture Library; 57: Franklin D Roosevelt Library/NARA; 59: Military Museum of Finland/Wikimedia/CC-BY-4.0; 61: Daily Mail /Shutterstock; 65: Bundesarchiv, Bild 101I-218-0504-36 / Dieck / CC-BY-SA 3.0; 67: AP/Shutterstock; 69: Anonymous/AP/Shutterstock; 71: National Archives and Records Administration, College Park; 73: National Archives and Records Administration, College Park; 75: National Archives and Records Administration, College Park; 77: Roger-Viollet/Shutterstock; 79: Bundesarchiv, Bild 141-0678 / CC-BY-SA 3.0; 81: Ian Forshaw/MOD; 83: AP/Shutterstock; 85: Ministry of the Navy; 87: Herbert Mason/Daily Mail/ Shutterstock; 91: Franklin D Roosevelt Library/NARA; 93: Augusto Ferrer Dalmau; 95: GL Archive/Alamy Stock Photo; 97: Lukasz Katlewa/ Wikimedia/CC-BY-3.0; 99: Library of Congress/Toni Frissell

collection; 101: FORTEPAN/Mihályi Balázs/Wikimedia/CC-BY-3.0; 103: Sem/Shutterstock; 105: Nationaal Archief, Netherlands; 107: National Archives and Records Administration, College Park; 109: AP/Shutterstock; 111: The Art Archive/Shutterstock; 113: Chronicle/Alamy Stock Photo; 117: National Museum of the US Navy; 119: Granger/Shutterstock; 121: Visem/Wikimedia/ CC-BY-3.0; 127: National Archives and Records Administration, College Park; 131: Oleg Konin/Shutterstock; 133: Granger/ Shutterstock; 137: Chronicle/Alamy Stock Photo 139: National Museum of the US Navy; 141: National Archives and Records Administration, College Park; 147: Pictorial Press Ltd/Alamy Stock Photo; 149: Sipa/Shutterstock; 151: AP/ Shutterstock; 153: United States Office of War Information; 155: Glasshouse Images/Shutterstock; 157: Library of Congress/Farm Security Administration - Office of War Information photograph collection; 159: Narodowe Archiwum Cyfrowe, Poland/Heinrich Hoffmann; 161: National Archives and Records Administration, College Park; 163: Roland Geider; 165: Adam Jones/Wikimedia/ CC-BY-2.5; 167: Adam Jones/Wikimedia/CC-BY-3.0; 169: National Archives and Records Administration, College Park; 173: Brian Jenkins/Wikimedia/CC-BY-3.0; 175: Steffen 692; 177: Library of Congress/Harris & Ewing, photographer. P. Street scenes, 1/39. District of Columbia United States Washington D.C.; 179: National Archives and Records Administration, College Park/ Office of War Information, Picture Division Library; 181: Franklin D Roosevelt Library/NARA Public domain Photographs; 183: National Archives and Records Administration, College Park; 185: Heritage Image Partnership Ltd/Alamy Stock Photo; 187: Daily Mail/Shutterstock; 189: National Archives and Records Administration, College Park; 191: Library of Congress/Farm Security Administration - Office of War Information photograph collection, photo by Howard R. Hollem; 193: National Archives and

Records Administration, College Park; 195: Library of Congress/ Farm Security Administration - Office of War Information photograph collection; 197: Library of Congress/Toni Frissell collection; 199: Library of Congress/Ansel Adams Photographs of Japanese-American Internment at Manzanar; 201: Universal History Archive/Shutterstock; 203: Japanese Army photo; 205: National Archives and Records Administration, College Park; 207: National Archives and Records Administration, College Park; 211: Associated Newspapers/Shutterstock; 213: National Archives and Records Administration, College Park/Records of the US Marine corps; 215: National Archives and Records Administration, College Park; 217: Australian War Memorial; 219: National Archives and Records Administration, College Park; 221: National Archives and Records Administration, College Park/ Official US Navy photograph; 223: National Archives and Records Administration, College Park/Official US Navy photograph; 225: United States Marine Corps; 227: National Museum of the US Navy; 229: Australian War Memorial; 231: US Army photo; 233: Xinhua News Agency/Shutterstock; 235: Thodra1/Wikimedia/CC-BY-4.0; 237: PumpkinSky/Wikimedia/CC-BY-4.0; 239: Universal History Archive/UIG/Shutterstock; 241: Bengal Speaks edited by Kalyanee Bhattacharyee, Hind Kitabs, Bombay, 1944 (first edition); 243: Associated Newspapers/Shutterstock; 245: National Archives, Kew/artist: Terenc Cuneo; 247: Bundesarchiv, Bild 101II-MW-3722-03 / Kramer / CC-BY-SA 3.0; 249: Library and Archives Canada / C-014160; 251: AP/Shutterstock; 253: Paul/Wikimedia/CC-BY-2.0; 255: LIFE Images Collection/Getty Images; 257: Conseil Régional de Basse-Normandie/National Archives USA; 259: United States Army Air Forces; 261: USAF; 263: Galerie Bilderwelt/Getty Images; 265: Bundesarchiv, Bild 183-H29758 / CC-BY-SA 3.0; 267: US Government photo; 269: USAF; 271: Deutsche Fotothek/Wikimedia/CC-BY-3.0; 273: Sergei Strunnikov; 275: Sovfoto/Universal Images Group/ Shutterstock; 277: Time Inc./ photograph by Gregory Weil; 279: RIA Novosti archive, image #1274 / RIA Novosti / CC-BY-SA 3.0; 281: Fotosearch/Stringer/Getty Images; 283: USAF; 287: USAMHI/WWII signal Corps Photograph Collection; 289: Library of Congress/Farm Security Administration - Office of War Information photograph collection; 291: Franklin D Roosevelt Library/NARA Public domain Photographs; 293: Chronicle/ Alamy Stock Photo; 295: Keystone/Getty Images; 297: Granger/ Shutterstock; 303: Sem/Universal Images Group/Shutterstock; 305: LAPI/Roger Viollet/Getty Images; 307: Library of Congress LC-USZ62-132795; 309: Library of Congress LC-USZ62-111201; 311: National Archives and Records Administration, College Park/Official US Navy photograph; 315: AlfvanBeem; 317: David Monniaux/Wikimedia/CC-BY-3.0; 319: Library of Congress/Farm Security Administration - Office of War Information photograph collection, photo by Jack Downey; 321: National Archives and Records Administration, College Park; 323: Bundesarchiv, Bild 146-1972-025-10 / CC-BY-SA 3.0; 325: National Archives and Records Administration, College Park; 327: Ra Boe/Wikipedia, Lizenz: CC BY-SA 3.0; 329: Roland Geider; 333: Jean Housen/ Wikimedia/CC-BY-SA-3.0; 337: Science History Images/Alamy Stock Photo; 339: National Archives and Records Administration, College Park; 341: National Archives and Records Administration, College Park; 345: AP/Shutterstock; 347: Bundesarchiv, Bild 183-H27992/Sönnke, Hans/CC-BY-SA 3.0; 349: National Archives and Records Administration, College Park; 351: Shutterstock; 353: Mil.ru/Wikimedia/CC-BY-4.0; 355: Granger/Shutterstock; 357: National Museum of the US Navy; 359: USMC Archives and Special collections; 361: US Navy Photo; 363: National Archives and Records Administration, College Park; 365: US Army photo; 367: National Archives and Records Administration, College Park/Official US Navy photograph; 369: NavSource; 373: United States Air Force Historical Research Agency; 375: National Museum of the US Navy; 377: Library of Congress LC-USZ62-77854; 379: World History Archive/Alamy Stock Photo; 381: Granger/Shutterstock; 383: National Archives and Records Administration, College Park; 385: National Archives and Records Administration, College Park/Harry S Truman Library; 387: National Archives and Records Administration, College Park/Office of War Information, Picture Division Library; 389: National Archives and Records Administration, College Park; 391: Janczikowsky/Wikimedia/CC-BY-3.0; 393: National Archives and Records Administration, College Park/Record Group 238: National Archives Collection of World War II War Crimes Records, 1933 – 1949; 395: National Photo collection of Israel, Photography Dept. Government Press Office/phot by Zoltan Kluger; 397: Granger/Shutterstock; 399: National Archives and Records Administration, College Park/Series: Photographs of Marshall Plan Activities in Europe and Africa, ca. 1948 - ca. 1989; 401: Universal History Archive/Shutterstock; 403: Granger/ Shutterstock; 405: USAF; 407: Sipa/Shutterstock.

16/16

First published in Great Britain in 2019 by
Quercus Editions Ltd
Carmelite House
50 Victoria Embankment
London EC4Y 0DZ

An Hachette UK company

Copyright © Quercus Editions Ltd 2019
Text by R.G. Grant

Edited by Anna Southgate
Designed by Dave Jones
Picture Research by Sally Claxton
Proofread by Rachel Mallig
Indexed by Helen Snaith

A CIP catalogue record for this book is available from
the British Library

PB ISBN 9781787477292
EBOOK ISBN 9781787477285

Every effort has been made to contact copyright
holders. However, the publishers will be glad to rectify
in future editions any inadvertent omissions brought
to their attention.

The picture credits constitute an extension to this
copyright notice.

10 9 8 7 6 5 4 3 2 1

Printed and bound in China